EPIDEMIOLOGY OF MENTAL DISORDERS
AND PSYCHOSOCIAL PROBLEMS

Personality disorders

G. de Girolamo
Division of Mental Health
World Health Organization
Geneva, Switzerland

J. H. Reich
Department of Psychiatry
Harvard and Brown Medical Schools
Brookline, MA, USA

World Health Organization
Geneva
1993

WHO Library Cataloguing in Publication Data

de Girolamo, G.
  Personality disorders / G. de Girolamo, J. H. Reich.
  (Epidemiology of mental disorders and psychosocial problems)
  1. Personality disorders – epidemiology 2. Personality disorders – classification. I. Series

ISBN 92 4 156160 2   (NLM Classification: WM 190)

The World Health Organization welcomes requests for permission to reproduce or translate its publications, in part or in full. Applications and enquiries should be addressed to the Office of Publications, World Health Organization, Geneva, Switzerland, which will be glad to provide the latest information on any changes made to the text, plans for new editions, and reprints and translations already available.

The designations employed and the presentation of the material in this publication do not imply the expression of any opinion whatsoever on the part of the Secretariat of the World Health Organization concerning the legal status of any country, territory, city or area or of its authorities, or concerning the delimitation of its frontiers or boundaries.

The mention of specific companies or of certain manufacturers' products does not imply that they are endorsed or recommended by the World Health Organization in preference to others of a similar nature that are not mentioned. Errors and omissions excepted, the names of proprietary products are distinguished by initial capital letters.

The authors alone are responsible for the views expressed in this publication. Where the designation "country or area" appears in the headings of tables, it covers countries, territories, cities, or areas.

TYPESET IN INDIA
PRINTED IN ENGLAND
93/9660–Macmillan/Clays–6000

Contents

Preface   v

Acknowledgements   ix

List of acronyms and abbreviations used in this book   x

1. Introduction   1

2. Diagnostic issues   2

   2.1 Definition of personality, personality trait and personality disorder   2
   2.2 Classification of personality disorders   3
   2.3 ICD-10, DSM-III and DSM-III-R classification of personality disorders   4
   2.4 Similarities and differences between ICD-10 and DSM-III-R   7
   2.5 Categorical versus dimensional styles of classification   8
   2.6 Controversial diagnostic categories   9
   2.7 Assessment methods for personality disorders   10

3. Epidemiology of personality disorders   15

   3.1 Incidence studies   15
   3.2 Prevalence studies   15
      Community surveys of unspecified personality disorders   15
      Community surveys of specific personality disorders   18
      Studies carried out in primary health care facilities   26
      Studies carried out in psychiatric settings   28
      Comorbidity of personality disorders   34
      Studies carried out in other institutions   37
   3.3 Temporal trends in the prevalence of personality disorders   37

4. Conclusions and recommendations for future studies   39

References   41

Annex 1

The ICD-10 Classification of Mental and Behavioural
Disorders: clinical descriptions and diagnostic guidelines
F60–F62 Specific personality disorders, mixed and
other personality disorders, and enduring personality
changes   54

Annex 2

The ICD-10 Classification of Mental and Behavioural
Disorders: diagnostic criteria for research
F60–F62 Specific personality disorders, mixed and
other personality disorders, and enduring personality
changes   61

Preface

Psychiatric illness is common and can have serious consequences. It has been estimated that as many as 500 million people may be suffering from some kind of mental disorder or impairment. In many countries 40% of disabled people owe their disability to mental disorders. Epidemiological predictions concerning mental illness show that there is every probability that the magnitude of mental health problems will increase in the future, as a result of various factors, including the increasing life expectancy of those with a mental disorder or disability and the growing number of people reaching the ages in which the risk of mental disorder is high.

The magnitude of mental health problems far exceeds that of the resources available for their resolution. In most parts of the world services which could help people who suffer from mental disorders are insufficient in both quality and quantity. This is often true even in the most highly developed countries. The general public and most of the professional medical community—often including psychiatrists—are insufficiently aware of the extent and nature of mental disorders and of the burden which these disorders represent for the individuals who suffer from them, their families and their communities. Traditional health statistical services in most countries are unable to provide accurate information about the extent of mental health problems in their populations. Most statistics routinely collected by health statistical services are based on mortality, which may lead to a distorted picture of the health status of a population since diseases of long duration that do not necessarily end in death—including many mental and neurological conditions—do not show up in such statistics. Lack of awareness of the magnitude and nature of mental health problems and of the availability of effective means of preventing or treating them is the cause of the low priority given to mental health programmes in most countries.

If health priorities are to be chosen properly, it is essential for accurate information to be available on the incidence and prevalence of mental and neurological disorders in the community and in general health facilities, their variation across countries and cultures and over time, their sociodemographic characteristics and the risk factors associated with their occurrence.

Unfortunately, reliable and comparable epidemiological data on mental and neurological disorders are scarce. Two of the reasons for the paucity of such data are particularly important: (1) the inadequacy of the training received by general health care personnel (and the absence of biological markers of mental illness) leads to a low recognition rate of mental health problems in their patients; and (2) the absence until recently of a "common language"—comprising a nomenclature, an agreed diagnostic system, and standardized instruments for the assessment of these disorders—means that the data that have been collected are not truly comparable.

Ideally, a series of cross-cultural surveys should be carried out for well-defined conditions or groups of conditions in order to advance our knowledge of the epidemiology of mental health problems. Over the past 20 years considerable progress has been made in developing the methodology for carrying out such work. WHO has played an important role in this field: with the publication of diagnostic guidelines (WHO, 1992a) accompanying Chapter V of the Tenth Revision of the *International Statistical Classification of Diseases and Related Health Problems* (ICD-10) (WHO, 1992b), a widely tested and accepted diagnostic system has become available; WHO has also contributed to the development of instruments for the standardized assessment of psychopathology, including the Composite International Diagnostic Interview (CIDI) (Robins et al., 1988), the Schedules for Clinical Assessment in Neuropsychiatry (SCAN) (Wing et al., 1990), and the International Personality Disorder Examination (IPDE) (Loranger et al., 1991), and developed a network of centres in which training in their use can be obtained. In addition, WHO has carried out cross-cultural clinical and epidemiological research which has demonstrated that such work is feasible, and established research teams and centres in which further related work can be carried out.

Some countries have conducted major epidemiological studies in recent years (e.g. Brazil, China, USA), but data on the epidemiology of mental disorders are still scarce and difficult to obtain. For these reasons, WHO decided to produce a series of monographs, each of which discusses epidemiological data on a specific disorder (or group of related disorders). Special attention is given to epidemiological data gathered in developing countries, which are often neglected in epidemiological reviews published in scientific journals. As shown in several major WHO epidemiological studies, e.g. the International Pilot Study of Schizophrenia (WHO, 1979); the study on depression in different cultures (Sartorius et al., 1983); the study on the determinants of the outcome of severe mental disorders (Jablensky et al., 1992); the study on pathways to psychiatric care (Gater et al., 1991); and the study on ill-defined psychological disorders in general medical settings (Sartorius et al., 1990), the comparison of epidemiological data obtained in developing countries, or in countries that do not have a long tradition of epidemiological research, with those gathered in developed countries, or in countries with a stronger tradition of such research, can provide valuable insights into the very nature of the disorders—their causes, form, course and outcome.

All these monographs are similar in format: they review issues related to diagnosis and classification, with special reference to ICD-10, as well as the standardized assessment instruments available and used for the assessment of mental disorders. Incidence and prevalence studies carried out in the general population, in primary care settings, and in psychiatric settings, as well as in other institutions such as nursing homes, prisons, etc., are also reviewed. The main risk factors for the disorder, or group of disorders, are then discussed, and data on time trends in the prevalence and incidence of the disorder given where available. Each monograph ends with conclusions and recommendations for future studies.

It is hoped that these monographs will help research and health institutions, health planners, clinicians, and those concerned with informing the general public to better understand the magnitude of the problems they have to face, to develop effective preventive strategies and to build appropriate and humane care-delivery systems.

References

Gater R et al. (1991) The pathway study. *Psychological medicine*, 21: 761–774.

Jablensky A et al. (1992) Schizophrenia: manifestations, incidence and course in different cultures. A World Health Organization ten-country study. *Psychological medicine*, Suppl. 20.

Loranger AW et al. (1991) The WHO/ADAMHA International Pilot Study of Personality Disorders: background and purpose. *Journal of personality disorders*, 5: 296–306.

Robins LN et al. (1988) The Composite International Diagnostic Interview. *Archives of general psychiatry*, 45: 1069–1076.

Sartorius N et al. (1983) *Depressive disorders in different cultures*. Geneva, World Health Organization.

Sartorius N et al., eds. (1990) *Psychological disorders in general medical settings*. Berne, Huber.

WHO (1979) *Schizophrenia: an international follow-up study*. Chichester, Wiley.

WHO (1992a) *The ICD-10 Classification of Mental and Behavioural Disorders. Clinical descriptions and diagnostic guidelines*. Geneva, World Health Organization.

WHO (1992b) *The International Statistical Classification of Diseases and Related Health Problems, tenth revision. Volume 1: tabular list*. Geneva, World Health Organization.

Wing JK et al. (1990) SCAN: Schedules for Clinical Assessment in Neuropsychiatry. *Archives of general psychiatry*, 47: 589–593.

Acknowledgements

The authors thank Professor A. S. Henderson, Social Psychiatry Unit, National Health and Medical Research Council, Australian National University, Canberra, Australia, for his invaluable comments during the preparation of this monograph. Thanks are also due to Professor P. Casey, Department of Psychiatry, University College, Dublin, Ireland; Professor A. W. Loranger, Department of Psychology, Westchester Division, The New York Hospital and Cornell Medical Center, White Plains, NY, USA; and Professor P. Tyrer, Department of Psychiatry, St Charles Hospital, London, England, for reviewing the manuscript and for their comments and suggestions.

List of acronyms and abbreviations used in this book

ADAMHA	Alcohol, Drug Abuse and Mental Health Administration
BPD	Borderline Personality Disorder Scale
BSI	Borderline Syndrome Index
CIDI	Composite International Diagnostic Interview
CIS	Clinical Interview Schedule
DIB	Diagnostic Interview for Borderline Patients
DIN	Diagnostic Interview for Narcissism
DIPD	Diagnostic Interview for Personality Disorders
DIS	Diagnostic Interview Schedule
DSM-I	*Diagnostic and Statistical Manual of Mental Disorders*, 1st ed.
DSM-II	*Diagnostic and Statistical Manual of Mental Disorders*, 2nd ed.
DSM-III	*Diagnostic and Statistical Manual of Mental Disorders*, 3rd ed.
DSM-III-R	*Diagnostic and Statistical Manual of Mental Disorders*, 3rd ed. (revised)
DSM-IV	*Diagnostic and Statistical Manual of Mental Disorders*, 4th ed.
ECA	European Catchment Area Program
GP	General practitioner
ICD-8	*Manual of the International Statistical Classification of Diseases, Injuries, and Causes of Death. Eighth Revision.*
ICD-9	*Manual of the International Statistical Classification of Diseases, Injuries, and Causes of Death. Ninth Revision.*
ICD-10	*International Statistical Classification of Diseases and Related Health Problems. Tenth Revision.*
IPDE	International Personality Disorder Examination
MCMI	Millon Clinical Multiaxial Inventory
NTS	Narcissistic Trait Scale
PAF	Personality Assessment Form
PAS	Personality Assessment Schedule
PD	Personality disorder
PDE	Personality Disorders Examination
PDQ	Personality Diagnostic Questionnaire
PDQ-R	Personality Diagnostic Questionnaire—Revised
PIQ-II	Personality Interview Questions II
PSE	Present State Examination
RDC	Research Diagnostic Criteria
SADS	Schedule for Affective Disorders and Schizophrenia
SADS-L	Schedule for Affective Disorders and Schizophrenia—Lifetime

SAP	Standardized Assessment of Personality
SCAN	Schedules for Clinical Assessment in Neuropsychiatry
SCID	Structured Clinical Interview for DSM-III Personality Disorders
SCID-II	Structured Clinical Interview for DSM-III-R Personality Disorders
SCID-PQ	Structured Clinical Interview for DSM-III-R Personality Disorders–Personality Questionnaire
SFS	Social Functioning Schedule
SIB	Schedule for Interviewing Borderlines
SIPD	Structured Interview for DSM-III Personality Disorders
SIPD-R	Structured Interview for DSM-III Personality Disorders—Revised
SNAP	Schedule for Normal and Abnormal Personality Disorders
SPE	Standardized Psychiatric Examination
TPQ	Tridimensional Personality Questionnaire
WISPI	Wisconsin Personality Inventory

1

Introduction

Despite the importance of personality in human functioning, it is only in recent years that the epidemiology of personality disorders (PDs) has been investigated, and that the first comprehensive reviews in English have been published (Casey, 1988; Merikangas, 1989; Merikangas & Weissman, 1986). The need to investigate the epidemiology of PDs is justified for several reasons: firstly, as shown by the most recent epidemiological surveys, PDs are common and have been found in different countries and sociocultural settings; secondly, PDs can be very detrimental to the life of the affected individual and highly disruptive to societies, communities and families; and, thirdly, personality status is often a major variable in predicting the outcome of other psychiatric disorders and their response to treatment (Andreoli et al., 1989; Reich & Green, 1991). Already in 1971, a WHO Seminar on Standardization of Psychiatric Diagnosis, dealing with PDs, recommended that "Epidemiological research should be conducted in the light of the sociocultural and particularly the cross-cultural and comparative aspects of this problem and its public health implication" (WHO, 1972).

This publication begins by discussing the main nosological problems related to PDs and the assessment methods, and goes on to review the epidemiological data on PDs. Finally, the main gaps in current knowledge are discussed and recommendations are made for future studies.

2

Diagnostic issues

2.1 Definition of personality, personality trait and personality disorder

Personality is defined in the second edition of the *Lexicon of psychiatric and mental health terms* (WHO, in press) as "The ingrained patterns of thought, feeling, and behaviour characterizing an individual's unique lifestyle and mode of adaptation, and resulting from constitutional factors, development, and social experience."

Personality trait (originally designated by Allport (1937) as "a constant or persistent way of behaving") is defined as "an ideal 'constant purposive portion' (Stern, 1921) of the personality which is inferred from the totality of an individual's behaviour but never directly observed. A trait is a stable attribute and is often compared and contrasted with state, which is a momentary or time-limited characteristic of an organism or a person" (WHO, in press). Trait therefore refers to "persistent, habitual and recurrent behaviours. The term 'trait' does not explain these regularities, it describes them" (Klerman & Hirschfeld, 1988). However, personality traits as recognized by the revised third edition of the *Diagnostic and statistical manual of mental disorders* (DSM-III-R) (American Psychiatric Association, 1987) are "prominent aspects of personality, and do not imply pathology".

There are two basic types of personality disorder included in the diagnostic guidelines (WHO, 1992a) accompanying Chapter V of the Tenth Revision of the *International Statistical Classification of Diseases and Related Health Problems* (ICD-10) (WHO, 1992b): early onset (long-term) and adult onset (enduring personality change). In the first draft of ICD-10, the category of "personality trait accentuation" was included, defined as "a personality aberration of lesser severity than personality disorder, in which the personality is disharmonious either because of a conspicuous exaggeration of a single trait, or because several traits are abnormally accentuated to a lesser degree. Trait accentuation itself is not a disorder and rarely leads to referral." Because of this last statement, it was decided not to include personality trait accentuation in ICD-10. As regards enduring personality change, this is defined as "a disorder of adult personality and behaviour that has developed following catastrophic or excessive prolonged stress, or following a severe psychiatric illness, in an individual with no previous personality disorder. There is a definite and enduring change in the individual's pattern of perceiving, relating to, or thinking about the environment and the self. The personality change is associated with inflexible and maladaptive behaviour that was not present before the pathogenic experience and is not a manifestation of another mental disorder or a residual symptom of any antecedent mental disorder" (WHO, in press).

Personality disorders, according to the ICD-10 diagnostic guidelines (WHO, 1992a), "comprise deeply ingrained and enduring behaviour patterns, manifesting themselves as inflexible responses to a broad range of personal and social situations. They represent either extreme or significant deviations from the way the average individual in a given culture perceives, thinks, feels, and particularly, relates to others. Such behaviour patterns tend to be stable and to encompass multiple domains of behaviour and psychological functioning. They are frequently, but not always, associated with various degrees of subjective distress and problems in social functioning and performance." For example, a dependent personality disorder in a favourable environment might not cause dysfunction, but nevertheless might be considered a disorder since it is clinically identical to the same disorder that usually causes dysfunction.

In general, almost all definitions of PD include three key concepts:

1. An onset in childhood or adolescence.
2. A long-standing persistence over time; however, it is not only the persistence over time, but also the pervasiveness of the abnormal behaviour pattern across a broad range of personal and social situations, that constitutes the most relevant feature.
3. The association with a substantial degree of personal distress and/or problems in occupational or social performance.

2.2 Classification of personality disorders

There has been considerable interest in the study of personality and personality disorders since early times. Already in the fourth century BC, the philosopher Theophrastus described different types of personalities in a way that resembles some modern classification systems (Adlington, 1925, quoted by Tyrer et al., 1991). In the psychiatric field, it was Pinel, in 1801, who first distinguished personality disorders ("manie sans délire") from mental illness. He used the term "manie sans délire" to refer to people who had no delusions but were prone to unexplainable, sudden violent behaviours. This definition was subsequently refined during the 19th century by several well-known psychiatrists such as Janet in France, Prichard & Maudsley in England, and Rush in the USA (Tyrer et al., 1991). Other classifications of types of personality and personality disorders were gradually developed in other languages, including Japanese, Russian and Spanish. In Germany, Kraepelin (1921) finally endorsed the term "psychopathic personality" in the 8th edition of his famous treatise, in which he described seven different types of personality disorder. Later in the 1930s in Scandinavia, Sjobring (1973) proposed a scheme to describe and characterize personality mainly based on four dimensions, called

3

"stability", "solidity", "validity" and "capacity". This model became widespread in Scandinavian countries.

However, as noted by Tyrer et al. (1991), "The categorization of personality disorder did not receive any firm support until the time of Schneider." Schneider (1923) regarded abnormal personalities as "constitutional variants that are highly influenced by personal experiences" and identified ten specific types or classes of "psychopathic personality". The classification system proposed by Schneider has deeply influenced subsequent classification systems (Tyrer et al., 1991). Of the ten types of PD identified by Schneider, eight are closely related to similar types of PD as classified in DSM-III (American Psychiatric Association, 1980).

For many years the lack of standardized diagnostic criteria was a major obstacle to the scientific study of PDs, especially to the study of their epidemiology. For this reason, in 1971, a WHO Seminar on Standardization of Psychiatric Diagnosis (WHO, 1972) recommended:

(a) the strengthening and/or initiation of research on standardization of diagnosis and classification of PDs and epidemiological data on them;
(b) the introduction of a multiaxial or multidimensional system of recording PDs;
(c) the consideration of possible culture-specific entities;
(d) the development of methods to record the severity of the disorder.

Since then, important developments in the field of classification have taken place, notably the production and the forthcoming introduction of ICD-10 (WHO, 1992b), following a major international collaborative effort involving some 195 centres in 55 countries, and the introduction of the DSM-III multiaxial classification system (American Psychiatric Association, 1980).

2.3 ICD-10, DSM-III and DSM-III-R classification of personality disorders

Table 1 lists the specific PDs as classified in ICD-10, ICD-9 (WHO, 1977), DSM-III-R and DSM-IV (American Psychiatric Association, in press), while Annexes 1 and 2 show respectively the ICD-10 diagnostic guidelines and the ICD-10 diagnostic criteria for research for these disorders.

The ICD-10 diagnostic guidelines stress that PD is "nearly always associated with considerable personal and social disruption" (WHO, 1992a). In the ICD-10 classification, which does not have a multiaxial system for the separate recording of the personality status, PD can be diagnosed together with any other mental disorder, if present. Although a multiaxial system for ICD-10 is being developed, this will not include a separate axis for PDs, as in DSM-III and DSM-III-R. On the contrary, PDs will be included in axis A, which is the axis for medical conditions; axis B will deal with the assessment of disability in social and occupational functioning and axis C with environmental factors relevant for the occurrence of the disorder(s). Each axis will contain as many

Table 1

Comparison of classification of personality disorders in ICD-9, ICD-10, DSM-III-R and DSM-IV

ICD-9	ICD-10	DSM-III-R	DSM-IV
Paranoid personality disorder	Paranoid personality disorder	Paranoid personality disorder	Paranoid personality disorder
Schizoid personality disorder	Schizoid personality disorder	Schizoid personality disorder	Schizoid personality disorder
Personality disorder with predominantly sociopathic or asocial manifestations	Dissocial personality disorder	Antisocial personality disorder	Antisocial personality disorder
(a) Explosive personality disorder (b) NA	Emotionally unstable personality disorder: (a) Impulsive type (b) Borderline type	(a) NA (b) Borderline personality disorder	(a) NA (b) Borderline personality disorder
Hysterical personality disorder	Histrionic personality disorder	Histrionic personality disorder	Histrionic personality disorder
Anankastic personality disorder	Anankastic personality disorder	Obsessive–compulsive personality disorder	Obsessive–compulsive personality disorder
NA	Anxious [avoidant] personality disorder	Avoidant personality disorder	Avoidant personality disorder
NA	Dependent personality disorder	Dependent personality disorder	Dependent personality disorder
Affective personality disorder Asthenic personality disorder	Other specific personality disorders	Passive–aggressive personality disorder Schizotypal personality disorder Narcissistic personality disorder Self-defeating personality disorder Sadistic personality disorder	NA Schizotypal personality disorder Narcissistic personality disorder NA NA Personality disorder not otherwise specified

diagnoses as are necessary to describe the patient's condition. Despite the importance given to behavioural manifestations for the classification and assessment of PDs, personality traits and attitudes are also considered when a diagnosis is made. In fact with regard to the diagnostic criteria for specific PDs, the ICD-10 diagnostic guidelines subdivide PDs "according to clusters of traits that correspond to the most frequent or conspicuous behavioural manifestations" (WHO, 1992a). As stressed by Widiger & Frances (1985a), the reliance on behavioural indicators can improve inter-rater reliability, which reduces the amount of inferential judgement required for the diagnosis, but it does not ensure that the same diagnosis will be made at different times. Moreover, the diagnosis of a PD cannot be based on a single behaviour, as any given behaviour has multiple causes (e.g. situational and role factors).

Until now, only one study has explored the diagnostic categories for PDs contained in ICD-10 (first draft) (Blashfield, 1991). This study, carried out among 177 American clinicians, found some degree of overlap between the different categories. However, when the authors compared the diagnostic categories in ICD-10 with those in DSM-III-R, they found that only anankastic (ICD) and obsessive–compulsive (DSM) PDs showed a high level of correspondence.

With regard to the American taxonomic system, a multiaxial classification system was first introduced in DSM-III. Subsequently, with the development of DSM-III-R, more than 100 changes in the classification of PDs have been introduced as compared with DSM-III (Gorton & Akhtar, 1990; Widiger et al., 1988). While the multiaxial and categorical style of classification has been maintained, the diagnostic criteria have been revised to form a list of symptoms for each PD, of which only a certain number are required for a diagnosis to be reached. This polythetic format contrasts with the monothetic format employed for some PDs in DSM-III (e.g. schizoid, avoidant, dependent and compulsive), which required each of several criteria to be present to make a diagnosis. In DSM-III-R, each category of PD consists of 7–10 criteria and the presence of 4–6 is required for diagnosis. The DSM-III-R contains 11 PDs (see Table 1) plus two new disorders (self-defeating PD and sadistic PD) which were not included in DSM-III and which are considered as diagnostic categories needing further study. As in DSM-III, the 11 PDs are divided into three clusters:

- Cluster A (the "odd" or "eccentric" cluster), which includes paranoid, schizoid and schizotypal PD.
- Cluster B (the "dramatic" or "erratic" cluster), which includes histrionic, narcissistic, antisocial and borderline PDs.
- Cluster C (the "anxious" cluster), which includes avoidant, dependent, obsessive–compulsive and passive–aggressive PDs.

One study in the USA has examined the impact of DSM-III-R on diagnostic practice and the internal consistency of the sets of criteria for PDs using a national sample of 291 patients who had been identified by their clinicians as manifesting personality disorders (Morey, 1988). The results demonstrated a substantial divergence between DSM-III and DSM-III-R diagnoses, especially evident for schizoid and narcissistic PDs; when DSM-III-R criteria were applied, there was an 800% increase in the rate of schizoid PD and a 350% increase in the rate of narcissistic PD diagnosed by the clinicians.

On the other hand, for some diagnostic categories, such as borderline PD, there was a good agreement between the two diagnostic systems. DSM-IV (American Psychiatric Association, in press) will include paranoid, schizoid, schizotypal, antisocial, borderline, histrionic, narcissistic, avoidant, dependent and obsessive–compulsive PDs as in the DSM-III-R classification, but with slight changes in the diagnostic criteria, as well as a new category "PD not otherwise specified". However, passive–aggressive, self-defeating and sadistic PDs (provisionally included in DSM-III-R) will not be included. The overall effect of these changes will be to increase the concordance between the DSM-IV and ICD-10 classification systems compared with that between the DSM-III-R and ICD-10. DSM-IV will also include the three clusters present in DSM-III-R.

2.4 Similarities and differences between ICD-10 and DSM-III-R

Table 1 shows that for seven categories of PD (paranoid, schizoid, dissocial/ antisocial, histrionic, anankastic/obsessive–compulsive, anxious/avoidant, and dependent), there is a specific correspondence between ICD-10 and DSM-III-R. For three categories, there are differences in nomenclature between the two systems; in particular, ICD-10 uses the term "anankastic" instead of "obsessive–compulsive", in order to avoid the erroneous implication of an inevitable link between this type of personality and obsessive–compulsive disorder. ICD-10 also uses the term "dissocial" instead of "antisocial", in order to prevent any possible connotation of stigmatization and the term "anxious" instead of "avoidant". Self-defeating PD, which is considered an independent diagnostic category in DSM-III-R, is included as a subcategory of dependent PD in ICD-10. Moreover, while DSM-III-R classifies borderline PD as a specific category, ICD-10 includes it as a subcategory of emotionally unstable PD. Narcissistic and passive–aggressive PDs (present in DSM-III-R) are included in ICD-10 under the category of "other specific PDs", which is absent in DSM-III-R. Finally, while DSM-III-R includes schizotypal PD as a PD, ICD-10 classifies it under "Schizophrenia, schizotypal and delusional disorders", to highlight the contiguity between this disorder and the schizophrenia group disorders, as shown by genetic and clinical studies. However, recent studies suggest that there may be a second type of schizotypal PD that is unrelated to schizophrenia (Torgersen, 1985).

In general terms, as observed by Kato (1988), there are three diagnostic categories of PD that have been consistently included in the classifications by Schneider (1923), Leonhard (1959), ICD-8, ICD-9, ICD-10, DSM-II, DSM-III, DSM-III-R and DSM-IV:

1. Paranoid PD.
2. Hysterical (or histrionic) PD.
3. Anankastic (or obsessive–compulsive) PD.

2.5 Categorical versus dimensional styles of classification

In general, researchers involved in the assessment of personality traits tend to use dimensional measures based on normal populations, whereas those concerned with personality types and, even more, clinicians concerned with PDs, tend to employ categorical concepts and assessment measures (Gorton & Akhtar, 1990).

The drawbacks of the categorical approach are: the difficulty of classifying patients who are at the boundary of different categories or who do not meet the diagnostic criteria for any specific PD but still have significant pathology; the need for heterogeneous categories, such as "mixed" and "atypical" cases; the need to simplify necessarily complex conditions; and the use of a nominal rather than an ordinal scale (Gorton & Akhtar, 1990). On the other hand, a dimensional approach may not be appropriate when dealing with severe clinical problems and may not permit findings from different cultures to be compared easily. Those in favour of a dimensional approach argue that PDs differ from normal variation in personality only in terms of degree, and to some extent this is supported by empirical data. For example, in a study carried out among 609 psychiatric outpatients using a 4-point rating scale for DSM-III axis II categories, 51% of the patients met the criteria for one or more PDs (Kass et al., 1985). The percentage rose to 88% when patients rated as having "some traits" or "almost meeting DSM-III criteria" were included. The authors conclude that the adoption of the current categorical approach would have caused the loss of important clinical information, especially for those less common disorders (e.g. narcissistic PD), for which milder forms are at least ten times more common than the disorders themselves. Widiger et al. (1987) also found evidence to support a dimensional model in a study carried out among 84 patients assessed for the presence of a PD.

Another recent study, carried out among a sample of 158 patients with a primary diagnosis of PD and a control sample of 274 general population volunteers, using self-report scales developed to measure 79 traits identified as representative of personality diagnoses, found a high degree of similarity between the traits resulting from factor analysis in the two samples (Schroeder & Livesley, 1991). This seems to suggest that the features of personality can be regarded as a continuum.

Moreover, it is still unclear whether normal and abnormal personality traits are the same or whether they are qualitatively different. Evidence for the latter includes: the fact that normal personality traits are at least moderately heritable while abnormal personality traits appear less heritable and that the prevalence rates of PDs found in surveys are much greater than would be expected from the prevalence rates of normal personality traits in the general population. Some researchers (e.g. Birtchnell, 1988) have even suggested that an extreme form of a normal personality trait is not necessarily pathological.

It is still unclear whether PDs are best characterized as dimensional or categorical because of lack of empirical evidence. However, it is possible that different models may be appropriate in different situations.

2.6 Controversial diagnostic categories

Some diagnostic categories of PD have raised important conceptual problems and have stimulated an active discussion among various researchers. They include borderline PD, passive–aggressive PD (included in DSM-III and DSM-III-R), histrionic PD, dissocial/antisocial PD, and sadistic PD and self-defeating PD (provisionally included in DSM-III-R).

Borderline PD has been, for many years, a questionable diagnostic concept. It did not appear in ICD-9 and the term was rarely used in Europe; on the other hand, it became quite popular in the USA. A recent review of over 70 papers published on this topic, mainly between 1980 and 1986, concluded that the weight of evidence supported the validity of this category (Tarnopolsky & Berelowitz, 1987). However, more recent studies have found that borderline PD constitutes a very heterogeneous category with unclear boundaries, overlapping with many different disorders but without a specific association with any of them (Fyer et al., 1988a; Nurnberg et al., 1991). In particular, a recent review has ruled out the existence of a specific relationship between borderline PD and depression (Gunderson & Phillips, 1991).

As regards passive–aggressive PD, it was included in DSM-I as a consequence of the experience gained in treating service personnel in the Second World War. After a long debate, this PD was included in DSM-III with the restrictive condition that it should not be diagnosed in the presence of any other PD, as some felt that this disorder could be a situational reaction to being powerless or a subordinate (Widiger et al., 1988). This exclusion criterion was not included in DSM-III-R.

Histrionic PD has also been criticized for compromising validity by including female social norms to diagnose women as having the disorder. The fact that histrionic PD is frequently diagnosed in women is used to support this conclusion. However, there is no evidence of this disorder being over-diagnosed by experienced clinicians. Moreover, it is not necessarily a sign of bias for a disorder to occur more in one sex; major depression is also more common in women, while dissocial PD is more common in men.

As discussed earlier, the concept of dissocial (antisocial) PD has been used for over 180 years (Lewis, 1974), yet it has remained a difficult concept, because of the difficulty of drawing a dividing line between normal and abnormal behaviour that is independent of local cultural values and societal norms. Blackburn (1988) has been the most critical exponent among those who have stressed the "normative" aspect of this diagnosis; he has suggested that the concept of dissocial PD "remains a 'mythical entity'... Such a concept is little more than a moral judgement masquerading as a clinical diagnosis. Given the lack of demonstrable scientific or clinical utility of the concept, it should be discarded." Similar views have been expressed by Lewis (1974) and Shepherd & Sartorius (1974), who stated that "antisocial personality disorder... is peculiarly susceptible to misunderstanding and misuse." Although the diagnosis of dissocial PD has the greatest empirical support and highest inter-rater reliability, it has been criticized for compromising validity for reliability by emphasizing easily identifiable criminal and delinquent behaviour. In particular, the DSM-III criteria for antisocial PD have been criticized because they do not give prominence to the traditional personality traits of psychopathy (e.g. incapacity to experience guilt, to learn from experience, or to maintain enduring relationships) and emphasize different aspects of criminality and irresponsibility. In addition, the diagnostic criteria are cumbersome. Similar problems have also been reported with the DSM-III-R criteria for antisocial PD (Hare et al., 1991; Widiger et al., 1991).

Sadistic PD was provisionally included in DSM-III-R mainly because of the need to evaluate patients who demonstrated a long-lasting maladaptive pattern of cruel, demeaning and aggressive behaviour towards others, but whose personality was not adequately described by any of the existing DSM-III categories of PD. Recently, a survey carried out among 279 members of the American Academy of Psychiatry and the Law found that approximately 50% of the respondents had, at some time, evaluated a person who met the criteria for sadistic disorder (Spitzer et al., 1991). Almost all the cases described involved male patients with a history of frequent abuse and loss of a parent during childhood. Most of the forensic psychiatrists who had experience with the disorder believed in the usefulness of the diagnosis for a variety of reasons. However, because of the lack of empirical data validating this diagnosis, it will not be included in DSM-IV (Pincus et al., 1992).

The category of self-defeating PD, also provisionally included in DSM-III-R, has been criticized on the grounds that it may be unwarranted, as many people who meet the criteria have been or are victims of abuse rather than instigators of it, and that it may be biased against victims of abuse. However, there have been reports that the disorder may be hereditary (Reich, 1988; Torgersen, 1989).

2.7 Assessment methods for personality disorders

Tables 2 and 3 show the main methods currently available for assessing all PDs and specific PDs. Some of the methods listed are new, while others have been revised two or three times (Reich, 1987a, 1989). The following points related to these methods need to be mentioned:

1. They have generally shown a satisfactory inter-rater reliability, while test–retest reliability has not been well established; however, two methods show reasonably good test–retest reliability—the Personality Assessment Schedule (PAS) (Tyrer et al., 1983) and the most recent version of the International Personality Disorder Examination (IPDE) (Loranger et al., 1991). It has been suggested that in the assessment of this particular group of disorders, the stability over time is especially important (Tyrer, 1987a, 1987b, 1990), as personality characteristics tend to be long-lasting.
2. Many of the methods have been standardized on psychiatric inpatient or outpatient populations; their applicability in epidemiological community studies is largely unknown.

Table 2

Assessment methods for all personality disorders

Name of method	Author(s)	Method of assessment	Number of items	Time required (mins)
Diagnostic Interview for Personality Disorders (DIPD)	Zanarini (1983)	Semistructured interview with patient using DSM-III-R criteria	101	60–120
International Personality Disorder Examination (IPDE)	Loranger et al. (1991)	Semistructured interview with patient using ICD-10 and DSM-III-R criteria	157	150
Millon Clinical Multiaxial Inventory (MCMI)	Millon (1982)	Self-report by patient using DSM-III-R criteria	175	20–30
Personality Assessment Schedule (PAS)	Tyrer et al. (1979)	Semistructured interview with informant(s) using DSM-III-R criteria	24	60
Personality Diagnostic Questionnaire—Revised (PDQ-R)	Hyler & Reider (1984)	Self-report by patient or informant(s) using DSM-III-R criteria	152	30
Personality Interview Questions II (PIQ-II)	Widiger (1987)	Semistructured interview with patient using DSM-III criteria	106	60–120
Schedule for Normal and Abnormal Personality Disorders (SNAP)	Clark (1989)	Self-report by patient using DSM-III and dimensional criteria	375	10
Standardized Assessment of Personality (SAP)	Pilgrim & Mann (1990)	Semistructured interview with informant(s) using ICD-10 and DSM-III-R criteria	NA	10–15
Structured Clinical Interview for DSM-III-R Personality Disorders (SCID-II)	Spitzer & Williams (1987)	Semistructured interview with patient using DSM-III-R criteria	120	60–90
Structured Interview for DSM-III Personality Disorders (SIPD)	Pfohl et al. (1983)	Semistructured interview with patient or informant(s) using DSM-III criteria	136	90
Tridimensional Personality Questionnaire (TPQ)	Cloninger (1987)	Self-report by patient	100	20–30
Wisconsin Personality Inventory (WISPI)	Klein (1985)	Self-report by patient using DSM-III criteria	360	20

Table 3
Assessment methods for specific personality disorders

Name of method	Author(s)	Personality disorder(s) covered	Method of assessment	Number of items	Time required (mins)
Borderline Personality Disorder Scale (BPD)	Perry (1982)	Borderline	Self-report by patient using DSM-III criteria	36	90
Borderline Syndrome Index (BSI)	Conte et al. (1980)	Borderline	Self-report by patient using DSM-III criteria	52	20–40
Diagnostic Interview for Borderline Patients (DIB)	Gunderson et al. (1981)	Borderline	Semistructured interview with patient or informant(s) using DSM-III criteria	165	90
Diagnostic Interview for Narcissism (DIN)	Gunderson et al. (1990)	Narcissistic	Semistructured interview with patient using DSM-III-R criteria	134	35–50
Diagnostic Interview Schedule (DIS)	Robins et al. (1981)	Antisocial	Semistructured interview with patient using DSM-III criteria[a]	44	40–90
Narcissistic Trait Scale (NTS)	Richman & Flaherty (1987)	Narcissistic	Self-report by patient using DSM-III criteria	10	less than 10
Schedule for Affective Disorders and Schizophrenia (SADS)	Endicott & Spitzer (1978)	Antisocial	Semistructured interview with patient or informant(s) using DSM-III criteria[a]	20	60–90
Schedule for Interviewing Borderlines (SIB)	Baron (1981)	Borderline; schizotypal	Semistructured interview with patient using DSM-III criteria	70	50

[a] Antisocial PD was the only PD generated by a larger interview schedule covering axis I disorders.

3. A main methodological problem is related to the choice of the person to be interviewed: many authors have argued that besides the patient a key informant should be interviewed as well, given the likelihood that many patients will not reply reliably to questions about their personality and the possibility that informant ratings will differ substantially from patient ones (Dodwell, 1988; Tyrer, 1987a; Zimmerman et al., 1988). However, even if an informant is interviewed, it is often not clear which source of information to believe in the case of disagreement and as yet there are no guidelines to solve the issue.

An important characteristic of some structured interviews is that they attempt to assess patients when they are not suffering from an axis I disorder;

however, when the latter disorder is chronic, this may be difficult to achieve (Tyrer, 1987a, 1987b). This problem also affects the ability of questionnaires to differentiate between current axis I disorders and PDs, as the self-judgement of patients who are suffering from a psychiatric condition is frequently impaired (Tyrer, 1987a).

In general, the agreement between clinicians' diagnoses of PDs and self-report measures is poor. A study comparing clinicians' diagnoses and self-report diagnoses obtained through the Personality Diagnostic Questionnaire (PDQ) among 552 patients found a very low agreement between the two measures: while the clinicians made an average of 0.7 diagnoses of PD per patient, the PDQ generated 2.4 diagnoses per patient (Hyler et al., 1989). Among patients suffering from a PD, the clinicians made 1.2 diagnoses per patient; by contrast, use of the PDQ resulted in an average of 3.0 diagnoses per patient. However, this result is not as serious as the lack of agreement between different methods of assessment, as shown in recent reports (Jackson et al., 1991a; Reich et al., 1987a).

Recently, Perry (1992) has reviewed the concordance between standardized interviews and self-report questionnaires for the diagnosis of PDs. On the basis of eight studies in which two or more diagnostic methods were used to assess patients for axis II disorders, the overall level of agreement between any two methods was low (median κ value $= 0.25$). The concordance between self-report questionnaires and standardized interviews was lower than between interviews. Perry (1992) concluded that current methods for the assessment of PDs have high reliability but that differences between those methods mean that the diagnoses are not comparable. The author suggested that the lack of concordance between methods was due to variations in raters, interview occasions, sources of information (patients or informants), the availability of historical clinical data, sensitivity to state effects (e.g. depression or anxiety may affect the prevalence of PDs using many current assessment methods), and format (e.g. methods that have a dichotomic format (yes/no) may fail to distinguish between sporadic occurrences and enduring patterns of behaviour). Perry (1992) has therefore proposed a different approach to the diagnosis of PDs, involving an interview with the patient, in which the occurrence of both axis I and axis II disorders during the patient's life is assessed. While this approach may prove to be effective, empirical studies will be required to determine its usefulness and validity.

In 1979, the WHO/ADAMHA Joint Program on the Diagnosis and Classification of Mental Disorders, Alcoholism, and Drug Abuse was established to foster a common language and improve the scientific basis of diagnosis and classification in the mental health field. As part of this programme, it was decided to develop a method for the diagnosis and assessment of PDs to be used at an international level to facilitate comparisons of clinical and research findings from different nations and cultures. This method, known as the IPDE (Loranger et al., 1991), is a standardized interview, which is arranged under six headings; (i) work; (ii) self; (iii) interpersonal relationships; (iv) affects; (v) reality testing; and (vi) impulse control. Its purpose is to assess the phenomena and life experiences relevant to the diagnosis of PDs in the ICD-10 and DSM-III-R classification systems.

The complexity of the method lies in the fact that it has to assess some 157 different diagnostic criteria pertaining to ICD-10 and DSM-III-R. The interview takes an average of 2.5 hours to complete. The scoring is on a three-point scale. With this method, for a behaviour to be considered a personality trait, it should exist for at least 5 years and at least one diagnostic criterion of the disorder must be fulfilled before the age of 25. The IPDE also has a second scoring column for data from informants. The IPDE has already been translated into 10 languages, and it is currently being tested in field trials in ten countries.

3

Epidemiology of personality disorders

3.1 Incidence studies

Because of the very nature of PDs, as discussed above (e.g. their chronic nature, their onset during childhood or adolescence, and the absence of an exact time of onset), it is theoretically very difficult to assess their incidence. However, there is one study that has assessed the lifetime expectancy of developing a PD. In a prospective survey of 5395 men and women in Iceland, born in 1895–97 and still alive in 1977, the expectancy rate was calculated on the basis of three assessments, made in 1957, 1971 and 1977 (Helgason & Magnusson, 1989). The expectancy rate of developing a PD before the age of 81 was 5.2%; however, this rate referred not only to PDs, but also to other unspecified disorders that did not meet diagnostic criteria for specific categories. In addition, the results were probably very much influenced by the fact that the people were not interviewed until they were 60 years of age or older.

3.2 Prevalence studies

Community surveys of unspecified personality disorders

Table 4 lists several community surveys in which the prevalence rate of unspecified PDs was calculated. Considering the studies where the diagnosis of PDs was based on only an unstructured clinical interview with the patient and/or a close informant, the prevalence rates range from 0.1%, found by Lin et al. (1989) in their survey in Taiwan, China and by Sethi et al. (1972) in their survey in a village in India, up to 9.8% found by Langner & Michael (1963) in the Midtown Manhattan Study in NY, USA, with a median rate of 2.8%. The rates seem lower for populations from developing countries. A very low rate of PD (0.01%) was also found in a national survey carried out in China (Cheung, 1991). However, the severe methodological limitations related to these studies (which were not specifically focusing on PDs) make the rates found hardly valid, comparable or generalizable because of differences in sampling methods, criteria for making diagnoses, the known unreliability of PD diagnoses based on clinical judgement and the fact that most of the studies did not use standardized assessment methods. In a review of 20 epidemiological studies of PDs carried out in psychiatric settings in Europe and North America since 1950, Neugebauer et al. (1980) found an average prevalence rate for PDs of

7%; however, their estimate also included alcohol dependence and drug abuse. Finally, in a recent review of epidemiological studies carried out in Latin America, Levav et al. (1989) found prevalence rates ranging from 3.4% (in Costa Rica) to 10.7% (in Peru), with a median rate of 4.7%.

Four studies recently published and aimed at ascertaining the prevalence rate of PDs in community samples or in relatives of patients with schizophrenia or depression using assessment methods specific for PDs (Casey & Tyrer, 1986; Maier et al., 1992; Reich et al., 1989a; Zimmerman & Coryell, 1990) have provided valuable epidemiological data; they will be briefly reviewed separately.

Table 4

Prevalence of personality disorders in epidemiological surveys

Author(s)	Country	Date of survey	Size of sample	Method of assessment [a]	Prevalence (%)
Allebeck et al. (1988)	Sweden	1969–70	50 465[b]	Clinical interview using ICD-8 criteria	2.7
Bash & Bash-Liechti (1987)	Islamic Republic of Iran	1963–70	1 468	Clinical interview using ICD-8 criteria[c]	1.0
Bremer (1951)	Norway	1939–44	1 080	Clinical interview using Scandinavian criteria	9.4
Casey & Tyrer (1986)	United Kingdom	NA	200[d]	PAS, PSE and SFS, using ICD-9 criteria	13.0
Dilling et al. (1989)	Germany	1975–79 1980–84	1 536 1 666	Clinical interview and CIS using ICD-8 criteria (1975–79), and ICD-9 and DSM-III-R criteria (1980–84)	0.7 2.8
Essen-Moller (1956)	Sweden	NA	2 550[e]	Clinical interview using ICD-8 criteria	6.4
Helgason (1981)	Iceland	1957–77	5 395	Clinical interview using Scandinavian criteria; informants	4.6
Langner & Michael (1963)	USA	1954	1 660	Clinical interview[f] using American criteria	9.8
Leighton (1959)	Canada	1952	1 010	Specific interview schedule[g] using DSM-I criteria	0.1
Lin et al. (1989)	China (Province of Taiwan)	1946–48 1961–63	19 931 39 024	Clinical interview using European criteria; informants	0.1 0.1

Table 4 *(cont.)*

Author(s)	Country	Date of survey	Size of sample	Method of assessment [a]	Prevalence (%)
Maier et al. (1992)	Germany	NA	447[h]	SCID using DSM-III criteria	10.3
Reich et al. (1989a)	USA	1985	235[i]	PDQ using DSM-III criteria	11.1
Sethi et al. (1972)	India	NA	2 691[j]	Clinical interview	0.1
Zimmerman & Coryell (1990)	USA	NA	697[k]	PDQ (a) and SIPD (b) using DSM-III criteria	(a) 10.3 (b) 13.5

[a] See page x.
[b] Refers to a survey of male military conscripts aged 18–20 years.
[c] Diagnoses were recoded using ICD-9 criteria.
[d] Refers to a survey carried out among patients selected at random from the practice lists of two general practitioners and interviewed at home.
[e] The Lundby study: a community survey of an entire population from Lund.
[f] The clinical interview was based on symptom questionnaires such as the Minnesota Multiphasic Inventory, the Cornell Medical Index and the World War II Screening Neuropsychiatric Adjunct.
[g] The interview schedule was partly based on the Health and Opinion Survey.
[h] Family study involving an unscreened control sample of 109 families.
[i] Adults randomly selected from a university community.
[j] Community survey carried out in a village.
[k] Sample included relatives of patients suffering from schizophrenia or depression.

In a random sample of 200 people selected from urban and rural communities in the United Kingdom and assessed with the PAS, 26 (13%) were found to have a PD (Casey & Tyrer, 1986). Explosive PD was the most common type of PD; there were no differences in prevalence between urban and rural samples, or between men and women. Among the 16 people (8%) identified as suffering from a mental disorder through the Present State Examination (PSE), more than half also had a PD. Social functioning was worse in those with PDs than in those with a normal personality; however, there were no significant differences between different categories of PD.

Maier et al. (1992) assessed an unscreened sample of 109 families in Germany for lifetime diagnoses of both axis I disorders and PDs. Among 447 people who were personally interviewed with the Schedule for Affective Disorders and Schizophrenia—Lifetime (SADS-L) and the Structured Clinical Interview for DSM-III-R Personality Disorders (SCID-II), they found a rate of PDs (10.3%) similar to that reported in the other three studies. The rates among males and females were 9.9% and 10.5% respectively, and were higher in younger than in older people. Significant associations between current axis I disorders and PDs were observed, in particular anxiety disorders with avoidant PD, and affective disorders with borderline PD.

In a community sample of 235 adults assessed with the PDQ, 26 (11.1%) were diagnosed as having a PD (Reich et al., 1988, 1989b). Among them, 12

17

(46%) were males and 14 (54%) were married; their mean age was 45.8 years. A history of alcohol abuse, unemployment and marital problems was more common among the group with PDs than among the controls. The age and sex distribution of DSM-III personality cluster traits was also assessed (Reich et al., 1989a); it was shown that traits in the schizoid cluster did not change with age, while traits in the dramatic and the anxious clusters had a significant association with age. Women aged 31–40 and men aged 18–30 had the highest levels of personality traits; however, women in this age group also had a higher mean number of traits than their male counterparts, with a corresponding increase in impairment.

In the study by Zimmerman & Coryell (1990), in which 697 relatives of psychiatric patients and healthy controls were assessed using the Structured Interview for DSM-III Personality Disorders (SIPD) and the PDQ, more individuals had a PD according to the SIPD (13.5% vs 10.3%). Schizotypal, histrionic, antisocial and passive–aggressive PDs were the most frequent diagnoses from the SIPD, while dependent PD was the most common using the PDQ. Multiple diagnoses were more frequent with the PDQ. The authors concluded that questionnaire and interview assessments of PDs generally show a poor concordance, and that the type of assessment can strongly affect the prevalence rate of the disorder found in the absence of a precise definition of it and of reliable external markers.

To summarize, in the four studies reviewed above, the prevalence rate found was substantially higher than in the previous surveys and generally consistent, ranging from 10.3% to 13.5%. These results suggest that the prevalence rate found is higher when more specific assessment methods are used.

In terms of the sociodemographic characteristics of people diagnosed as having a PD, the prevalence rate is higher in urban populations and lower socioeconomic groups. It also seems to vary between different age groups, with a slight decrease in older groups. Although the sex ratio is different for specific types of PDs, these differences tend to cancel each other out, with total rates of PDs being about equal for the two sexes.

Community surveys of specific personality disorders

Table 5 lists the prevalence rates for specific PDs. The majority of these estimates come from the studies by Maier et al. (1992), Reich et al. (1989a) and Zimmerman & Coryell (1990). In addition, data on the prevalence of some specific PDs have been reported by Baron et al. (1985), who assessed 750 first-degree relatives of probands with chronic schizophrenia ($n = 376$) and normal control probands ($n = 374$) using the Schedule for Affective Disorders and Schizophrenia (SADS) and the Schedule for Interviewing Borderlines (SIB). The authors concluded that stereotypal and paranoid PDs are genetically related to schizophrenia.

Table 5

Prevalence of specific personality disorders in epidemiological surveys[a]

Type of personality disorder	Author(s)	Country	Size of sample	Method of assessment[b]	Prevalence (%)
Avoidant	Baron et al. (1985)	USA	376[c]	SIB; SADS-L	1.6[c]
			374[d]		0[d]
	Maier et al. (1992)	Germany	447	SCID	1.1
	Reich et al. (1989a)	USA	235[d]	PDQ	0[d]
	Zimmerman & Coryell (1990)	USA	697	PDQ	0.4
				SIPD	1.3
Borderline	Baron et al. (1985)	USA	376[c]	SIB; SADS	1.9[c]
			374[d]		1.6[d]
	Maier et al. (1992)	Germany	447	SCID	1.1
	Reich et al. (1989a)	USA	235	PDQ	1.3
	Swartz et al. (1990)	USA	1541	DIB; DIS	1.8
	Zimmerman & Coryell (1990)	USA	697	PDQ	4.6
				SIPD	1.7
	Weissman & Myers (1980)	USA	511	SADS-L	0.2
Compulsive	Maier et al. (1992)	Germany	447	SCID	2.2
	Nestadt et al. (1991)	USA	759	SPE	1.7
	Reich et al. (1989a)	USA	235	PDQ	6.4
	Zimmerman & Coryell (1990)	USA	697	PDQ	4.0
				SIPD	1.7
Dependent	Baron et al. (1985)	USA	376[c]	SIB; SADS-L	0.3[c]
			374[d]		0[d]
	Maier et al. (1992)	Germany	447	SCID	1.6
	Reich et al. (1989a)	USA	235	PDQ	5.1
	Zimmerman & Coryell (1990)	USA	697	PDQ	6.7
				SIPD	1.7
Histrionic	Maier et al. (1992)	Germany	447	SCID	1.3
	Nestadt et al. (1990)	USA	810	SPE	2.1
	Reich et al. (1989a)	USA	235	PDQ	2.1
	Zimmerman & Coryell (1990)	USA	697	PDQ	2.7
				SIPD	3.0
Narcissistic	Maier et al. (1992)	Germany	447	SCID	0
	Reich et al. (1989a)	USA	235	PDQ	0.4
	Zimmerman & Coryell (1990)	USA	697	PDQ	0.4
				SIPD	0
Paranoid	Baron et al. (1985)	USA	376[c]	SIB; SADS-L	7.3
			374[d]		2.7
	Maier et al. (1992)	Germany	447	SCID	1.8
	Reich et al. (1989a)	USA	235	PDQ	0.8
	Zimmerman & Coryell (1990)	USA	697	PDQ	0.4
				SIPD	0.4
Passive–aggressive	Maier et al. (1992)	Germany	447	SCID	1.8
	Reich et al. (1989a)	USA	235	PDQ	0
	Zimmerman & Coryell (1990)	USA	697	PDQ	0.4
				SIPD	3.0

Table 5 (cont.)

Type of personality disorder	Author(s)	Country	Size of sample	Method of assessment[b]	Prevalence (%)
Schizoid	Baron et al. (1985)	USA	376[c]	SIB; SADS-L	1.6
			374[d]		0
	Maier et al. (1992)	Germany	447	SCID	5.1
	Reich et al. (1989a)	USA	235	PDQ	0.8
	Zimmerman & Coryell (1990)	USA	697	PDQ	0.9
				SIPD	0.7
Schizotypal	Baron et al. (1985)	USA	376[c]	SIB; SADS-L	14.6
			374[d]		2.1
	Maier et al. (1992)	Germany	447	SCID	0.6
	Reich et al. (1989a)	USA	235	PDQ	5.1
	Zimmerman & Coryell (1990)	USA	697	PDQ	5.6
				SIPD	3.0

[a] Adapted in part from Weissman (1993).
[b] See page x.
[c] First-degree relatives of patients with chronic schizophrenia.
[d] First-degree relatives of normal control probands.

Paranoid personality disorder

The prevalence of paranoid PD was first investigated by Leighton (1959) in the Stirling County Study and by Langner & Michael (1963) in the Midtown Manhattan Study, who reported markedly different rates of 0.03% and 28.4% respectively. Reich et al. (1989a) and Zimmerman & Coryell (1990) found comparable rates (0.4–0.8%), while Maier et al. (1992) reported a slightly higher rate (1.8%). On the other hand, Baron et al. (1985) found a significantly higher rate of paranoid PD among relatives of probands with chronic schizophrenia (7.3%) than among relatives of control probands (2.7%). This disorder seems to be more frequent in lower socioeconomic groups.

Schizoid personality disorder

In the Midtown Manhattan Study, Langner & Michael (1963) found a very high rate of schizoid PD (15.2%); however, much lower rates (0.4–0.9%) were reported by Maier et al. (1992), Reich et al. (1989a) and Zimmerman & Coryell (1990). Baron et al. (1985) reported a rate of 1.6% of schizoid PD among relatives of probands with chronic schizophrenia compared with no cases among relatives of control probands.

Schizotypal personality disorder

Family studies (in particular, the Danish Adoption Study) have helped in the understanding of the etiology and epidemiology of schizotypal PD. For this disorder, Reich et al. (1989a) and Zimmerman & Coryell (1990) reported rates (3.0% and 5.6% respectively) similar to that found by Langner & Michael (1963) in the Midtown Manhattan Study (4.9%); however, Maier et al. (1992) reported a rate of only 0.6%. The rates found employing similar assessment methods such as the PDQ are strikingly similar in spite of differences in sample characteristics, size and response rate. In the study by Baron et al. (1985), schizotypal PD was much more frequent among relatives of probands with chronic schizophrenia (14.6%) than among relatives of control probands (2.1%). This result provides further evidence for the existence of a specific relationship between schizophrenic disorders and schizotypal PD.

Histrionic personality disorder

In the Stirling County Study (Leighton, 1959), under the label of "emotionally unstable character", 2.2% of the adults were diagnosed as suffering from histrionic PD; the rate among women was twice that among men. Similar rates (1.3–3.0%) were reported by Maier et al. (1992), Nestadt et al. (1990), Reich et al. (1989a) and Zimmerman & Coryell (1990).

The study by Nestadt et al. (1990) was carried out as part of the Epidemiological Catchment Area Program (ECA) in Baltimore, MD, USA, and was aimed at ascertaining the prevalence of histrionic PD in the community. The authors found a prevalence of 2.2% for histrionic PD in the general population, with rates of 2.1% and 2.2% in men and women respectively. No significant differences were found in terms of race and education; however, the prevalence was significantly higher among separated and divorced persons than among married persons. In addition, 17% of the women with histrionic PD were also suffering from a depressive disorder. The rate of suicide attempts was higher in the group with histrionic PD, and these individuals were using medical services four times as often as those with a non-histrionic PD or the general population. Although histrionic personality traits were common in the general population, their frequency decreased as the number of traits increased, and those diagnosed as suffering from histrionic PD using DSM-III criteria were at the extreme end of the range. However, it should be noted that the authors of this study derived a secondary diagnosis from data which originally were not intended to diagnose personality.

Narcissistic personality disorder

Reich et al. (1989a) and Zimmerman & Coryell (1990), using the PDQ, found identical rates of narcissistic PD (0.4%). On the other hand, no cases were found by Maier (1992), using the Structured Clinical Interview for DSM-III Personality Disorders (SCID), or by Zimmerman & Coryell (1990), using the SIPD.

Borderline personality disorder

Borderline PD has been one of the most studied PDs. Weissman & Myers (1980), using the SADS-L and Research Diagnostic Criteria (RDC), reported a rate of only 0.2% among a sample of 511 adults in New Haven, CT, USA. However, they assessed a point and not a lifetime prevalence rate and this might explain the low rate.

Reich et al. (1989a), using the PDQ, reported a rate of 1.3%, while Zimmerman & Coryell (1990) reported rates of 4.6% using the PDQ and 1.7% using the SIPD; the latter rate was similar to that reported by Maier et al. (1992) of 1.1%. Furthermore, Zimmerman & Coryell (1990) found a high correlation between borderline PD and other PDs. When compared with individuals suffering from other PDs, persons with borderline PD also exhibited higher rates of alcohol abuse, tobacco use, phobic disorders, suicide attempts and schizophrenia. However, those with borderline PD were the youngest group, the least likely to be married and those who had married were either divorced or separated.

Swartz et al. (1990), using a diagnostic algorithm derived from the Diagnostic Interview Schedule or DIS (the DIS/Borderline Index), found a rate of 1.8% among 1541 adults (19–55 years of age) in the community at the Duke site of the ECA programme. Borderline PD was significantly more common among women, and among people who were either widowed or unmarried; rates were also higher among younger, non-white people and among those living in urban areas and belonging to lower socioeconomic groups. The highest rates were found in the 19–34 years age range, with the rates declining with age. Among the group with borderline PD, 98% had been given a diagnosis in the past year, and all had been given a lifetime diagnosis based on the DIS. Approximately half of the group had also been in contact with outpatient mental health services in the past 6 months. On the other hand, they did not use outpatient general health services more than the general population. Borderline PD was significantly related to a poor marital relationship, physical disability, job difficulties, alcohol-related problems, and psychosexual problems.

Although some psychiatrists have argued that borderline PD is more common among women than men, they have not adjusted for the underlying proportion of women in the studied populations (Akhtar et al., 1986; Widiger & Weissman, 1991). Carried to its extreme, this argument would say that it is legitimate to infer an excess of females in borderline populations by studying only female samples. However, several large studies have found no significant differences in prevalence between men and women (Kass et al., 1985; Reich, 1987b).

Dissocial (antisocial) personality disorder

Dissocial PD is one of the most studied PDs, and its prevalence has been assessed in a number of large-scale epidemiological surveys; those carried out prior to the introduction of ICD-10 and DSM-III are listed in Table 6. The median prevalence rate found in these studies is 4%. Since then many other studies, employing standardized diagnostic criteria, have been carried out and they are shown in Table 7.

In the ECA study, the prevalence of antisocial PD was specifically investigated: 1-month, 6-month and lifetime prevalence rates of respectively 0.5%, 1.2% and 2.6% were found, with a variation in the lifetime prevalence rate between the three sites from 2.1% to 3.4% (Robins & Regier, 1991). The

Table 6

Prevalence of dissocial personality disorders in epidemiological surveys prior to the introduction of ICD-10 and DSM-III[a]

Author(s)	Country	Size of sample	Prevalence (%)
Stromgren (1950)	Denmark	45 930	0.5
Bremer (1951)	Norway	1 325	9.4
Essen-Moller (1956)	Sweden	2 550	5.6
Langner & Michael (1963)	USA	1 911	1.9
Leighton (1959)	Canada	1 010	4.0
Helgason (1981)	Iceland	5 395	4.0

[a] Adapted from Weissman (1993).

lifetime prevalence rate for males was significantly higher (4.5%) than for females (0.8%), irrespective of age or ethnic group. This disorder was most common among people under the age of 45, among urban residents and among those who entered high school but did not complete it. The average duration of the disorder was 19 years, and its typical appearance was at the age of eight together with a variety of problems at home and in school. Less than half of the group with the disorder had a criminal record; however, job difficulties were reported in 94%, violence in 85%, and severe marital difficulties in 67%. In addition, 84% of the group had been engaged in some form of substance abuse; strong associations with schizophrenia and mania were also found (Regier et al., 1990).

In the Christchurch Psychiatric Epidemiologic Study, carried out in New Zealand using assessment methods similar to those employed in the ECA study, 6-month and lifetime antisocial PD prevalence rates of respectively 0.9% and 3.1% were found among a sample of 1498 adults aged 18–64 years (Wells et al., 1989). The disorder was more common among men than women (1.3% vs 0.5% for the 6-month prevalence rate and 4.2% vs 0.5% for the lifetime prevalence); however, these differences were not statistically significant, probably because of the limited size of the sample. The one-year recovery rate, defined as the percentage of persons who had ever met DSM-III criteria for the disorder and who had not experienced an episode or key symptoms relevant for that disorder in the past year, was 51.6%. However, it is possible that there was a distortion of state effects on PD diagnosis, and that many of those diagnosed and having recovered were drug abusers who no longer showed symptoms of antisocial PD after a period of abstinence.

In the Edmonton study, 3258 randomly selected adults were interviewed using the DIS (Bland et al., 1988a, 1988b); a lifetime prevalence rate of PDs of 33.8% was found. A prevalence rate of 3.7% (6.5% for males and 0.8% for females) was found for antisocial PD. The prevalence rate was highest in the age group 18–34 years, and among individuals who were widowed, separated or divorced. The mean age of onset reported was 7.6 years for males and 9.2 years for females; in all cases, onset had occurred before 20 years of age.

Table 7

Lifetime prevalence of antisocial personality disorders (DSM-III) in epidemiological surveys

Author(s)	Country or area	Size of sample	Method of assessment[a]	Prevalence (%)
Baron et al. (1985)	USA	376[b] 374[c]	SIB; SADS	0.5 0
Bland et al. (1988a, 1988b)	Canada	3 258	DIS	3.7
Chen et al. (1993)	Hong Kong	7 229	DIS	2.78 (males) 0.53 (females)
Hwu et al. (1989)	China (Taiwan)	11 004	DIS	0.03–0.14
Kinzie et al. (1992)	USA (Indian village)	131	SADS-L	1.4
Koegel (1988)	USA	328	DIS	20.8
Lee et al. (1990)	Republic of Korea	3 134 (urban) 1 966 (rural)	DIS	2.1 0.9
Maier et al. (1992)	Germany	447	SCID	0.2
Reich et al. (1989a)	USA	235	PDQ	0.4
Robins & Regier (1991)	USA (ECA Program)	18 571	DIS	2.1–3.4
Weissman & Myers (1980)	USA	511	SADS-L	0.2[d]
Wells et al. (1989)	New Zealand	1 498	DIS	3.1
Zimmerman & Coryell (1990)	USA	697	PDQ SIPD	0.9 3.0

[a] See page x.
[b] First-degree relatives of patients with chronic schizophrenia.
[c] First-degree relatives of normal control probands.
[d] Current prevalence of antisocial PD.

In Taiwan, China, the rates of antisocial PD were considerably lower, ranging from 0.03% in rural villages to 0.14% in metropolitan Taipei (Hwu et al., 1989). However, this is consistent with the rates reported for other DSM-III disorders in the Taiwan site. Similarly, Kinzie et al. (1992), using the SADS-L, reported a rate of 0.8% (one case among men; no cases among women) in a survey carried out among 131 adults living in an Indian village in western America.

Reich et al. (1989a) and Zimmerman & Coryell (1990), using the PDQ, also reported low rates of 0.4% and 0.9% respectively. However, the rates increased to 3.0% in the latter study when interviewers were used, suggesting that self-reports may underestimate the prevalence of antisocial PD. Maier et al. (1992), using a structured interview, also found a low rate of this disorder (0.2%).

Interesting results have been obtained by Koegel et al. (1988), in a survey carried out among 328 homeless individuals living in inner Los Angeles, CA, USA; they were assessed with the DIS, which had been modified to make it more sensitive for use with a homeless population. An overall lifetime rate of 20.8% of antisocial PD was found, as compared with a rate of 4.7% found in the Los Angeles sample included in the ECA study ($n = 3055$) (Robins & Regier, 1991); the risk ratio of suffering from antisocial PD in the homeless sample compared with the ECA sample was 4.4. However, the difference in rates was even more striking when the 6-month prevalence rate was considered: the rate among the homeless was 17.4% compared with 0.8% in the ECA sample, giving a risk ratio of 21.8.

To summarize, antisocial PD has been consistently found at a prevalence rate of 3% in the general population, more frequently among males than among females, with sex ratios ranging from 2:1 to 7:1; it is more common among younger adults, among people living in urban areas and among lower socioeconomic groups. In addition, people with antisocial PD exhibit high rates of contact with medical services.

Avoidant personality disorders

Baron et al. (1985) and Reich et al. (1989a) found no cases of avoidant PD among relatives of control probands, and Zimmerman & Coryell (1990) reported rates ranging from 0.4% (using the PDQ) to 1.3% (with the SIPD). The rate reported by Maier et al. (1992) (1.1%) was similar to that obtained by Zimmerman & Coryell (1990) and by Baron et al. (1985) among relatives of probands with chronic schizophrenia (1.6%).

Dependent personality disorders

In the Midtown Manhattan Study, 2.5% of the sample studied was diagnosed as suffering from passive–dependent PD (Langner & Michael, 1963). It was more common in women than in men, with an approximate sex ratio of 3:1. In the Stirling County Study, 0.9% of the sample exhibited a passive–aggressive or a passive–dependent pattern of behaviour (Leighton, 1959). Reich et al. (1989a) and Zimmerman & Coryell (1990), using the PDQ, reported rates of 5.1% and 6.7% respectively; however, lower rates (1.6% and 1.7%) were reported when structured interviews were used (Maier et al., 1992; Zimmerman & Coryell, 1990).

Obsessive–compulsive personality disorder

Reich et al. (1989a) and Zimmerman & Coryell (1990), using the PDQ, found comparable rates of obsessive–compulsive PD (6.4% and 4.0% respectively);

lower rates (2.2% and 1.7%) were reported when a structured interview was used (Maier et al., 1992; Zimmerman & Coryell, 1990). In another study carried out in the framework of the ECA in the Baltimore site, aimed at ascertaining the prevalence of compulsive PD (Nestadt et al., 1991) in the community, a prevalence of 1.7% was found. The prevalence rate among males was 3%, about five times that among females. The disorder was also more common among married white people who were employed and had been educated to university level. Persons with the disorder were considered to be at high risk of developing anxiety disorders. However, the authors of this study derived their diagnoses from data which originally were not intended to diagnose personality. This might explain why the authors found that the people with the disorder had a high incidence of marriage, high income and high social status, which are sociodemographic features not associated with PD. It is also possible that the authors identified people with adaptive obsessive–compulsive traits rather than those with obsessive–compulsive disorder.

Passive–aggressive personality disorder

In the Stirling County Study (Leighton, 1959), 0.9% of the sample exhibited a passive–aggressive or passive–dependent pattern of behaviour; however, that figure does not necessarily represent the prevalence of passive–aggressive PD itself. Using the PDQ, Zimmerman & Coryell (1990) found a low rate (0.4%), while Reich et al. (1989a) reported no cases among 235 volunteers. The rate was higher (1.8–3%) when direct interview was used (Maier et al., 1992; Zimmerman & Coryell, 1990), which suggests that persons with this disorder may under-report on self-report measures.

Studies carried out in primary health care facilities

Few studies have assessed the prevalence of PDs among users of medical services and, in particular, among users of primary health care services. In some studies, PDs have been classified under broader diagnostic categories, such as neurosis, making it impossible to estimate specific rates for PDs.

Kessel (1960) found that, among patients consulting their general practitioners, 5% were diagnosed as having abnormal personalities. In a larger study, Shepherd et al. (1966) found a similar prevalence rate and a higher rate among males than among females. In a sample of chronic psychiatric patients assessed in a primary health care setting, Cooper (1965) found that the psychiatrist identified 8% as having a primary diagnosis of a PD, while the general practitioner identified only 3%. In these studies psychiatric disorders and PDs were considered as mutually exclusive.

In one of the first studies carried out in a primary health care setting using a standardized interview, Cooper (1972) found a prevalence rate of 6.0% of PDs (7.1% in males and 5.7% in females) among 115 patients recognized as suffering from a psychiatric disorder.

In another survey, carried out among 2743 patients who consulted their general practitioner over a 12-month period, a 7% prevalence rate of psychiatric illness was found (Casey et al., 1984). Among the patients referred to a psychiatrist, 171 were assessed using the 9th edition of the PSE and the PAS. While in 8.9% of patients diagnosed by their general practitioner and 6.4% of those diagnosed by the interviewer as suffering from a psychiatric disorder, PD was regarded as the primary diagnosis, 33.9% of patients were assessed by the PAS as suffering from a PD. Explosive PD was the most frequently diagnosed PD, and the diagnosis of PD was linked to the diagnosis of anxiety states. At a 3-year follow-up assessment of over 80% of the original sample, the patients originally diagnosed as suffering from a PD showed greater morbidity, more contacts with all levels of psychiatric services and a higher consumption rate of psychotropic drugs, especially benzodiazepines (Seivewright et al., 1991).

Mann et al. (1981) found that, among 87 patients diagnosed by their general practitioner as suffering from non-psychotic disorders and subsequently interviewed with the Clinical Interview Schedule (CIS) and the Standard Assessment of Personality (SAP), 52 had certain features characteristic of PDs. Of these 52 patients, 31 were graded as having abnormal personalities.

In the framework of the Upper Bavarian studies, 1274 patients attending 18 general practitioners were assessed with the CIS by a psychiatrist; 32% of them were recognized as suffering from a specific mental disorder, and 26% were diagnosed according to the judgement of the general practitioner (Dilling et al., 1989). A total of 9.4% of the identified patients (equivalent to 3.3% of the original sample) were diagnosed by the psychiatrist as suffering from a PD; the percentage was higher among males (11.8%) than among females (8.1%).

In a recent study, 118 patients with somatization disorder were assessed for the presence of antisocial PD with the DIS and the SCID-II (Smith et al., 1991); 8% of the women and 25% of the men were diagnosed as suffering from antisocial PD, compared with 0.5–1.5% and 3.9–5.9% respectively in the general population. These data provide further evidence for an association between antisocial PD and somatization disorder.

The above studies indicate that, among patients attending primary health care facilities, 5–8% are identified by their general practitioner as having a primary diagnosis of PD. Prevalence rates appear to be higher among men than women. When the assessment is made independently of the primary diagnosis, however, the average prevalence rate can rise several-fold because of state effects. There are also indications that people showing certain PDs are among the highest users of medical services. For instance, in a community survey of 249 randomly selected volunteers, 10.4% of whom met DSM-III criteria for PDs, it was found that hospital admission rates over the past year were higher among patients with a PD than among controls (38% and 17% respectively) (Reich et al., 1989b). However, on another measure (a visit for a medical problem in the past year), there was no significant difference between the two groups.

Studies carried out in psychiatric settings

Table 8 lists the main epidemiological surveys of PDs carried out among patients in psychiatric settings. While it is clear that the prevalence of PDs among psychiatric outpatients and inpatients may be high, both in terms of patients showing only a PD and in terms of patients suffering from both an axis

Table 8

Prevalence of personality disorders among psychiatric patients in epidemiological surveys

Author(s)	Country	Size of sample	Method of assessment[a]	Prevalence (%)
Allan (1991)	United Kingdom	100 (outpatients)[b]	Clinical interview using Research Diagnostic Criteria	5.0
Alnaes & Torgersen (1988a, 1988b)	Norway	298 (outpatients)	SIPD using DSM-III criteria	81[c]
Baer et al. (1990)	USA	96 (outpatients)[d]	SIPD using DSM-III criteria	52[d]
Berger (1985)	Canada	486 (outpatients)[e]	Clinical assessment using DSM-III criteria	39
Castaneda & Franco (1985)	USA	1583 (inpatients)[f]	Clinical assessment using DSM-III criteria	6.4
Charney et al. (1981)	USA	160 (inpatients): (a) 64 with unipolar non-melancholic depression; (b) 66 with unipolar melancholic depression; (c) 30 with bipolar depression	Clinical assessment using DSM-III criteria	(a) 61 (b) 14 (c) 23
Cutting et al. (1986)	United Kingdom	100 (inpatients)[g]	SAP using Research Diagnostic Criteria	44.0[g]
Dowson & Berrios (1991)	United Kingdom	74 (21 inpatients; 53 outpatients)	PDQ-R using DSM-III-R criteria	NA[h]
Fabrega et al. (1993)	USA	18 179 (outpatients)	Initial evaluation form using DSM-III criteria	12.9[i]
Friedman et al. (1983)	USA	53 (inpatients)[j]	Clinical assessment using DSM-III criteria	87
Fyer et al. (1988a)	USA	(a) 598 (inpatients) (b) 501 (inpatients)[k]	Review of patients' medical records using DSM-III criteria	(a) 54.0 (b) 54.3[k]

Table 8 (cont.)

Author(s)	Country	Size of sample	Method of assessment[a]	Prevalence (%)
Hyler & Lyons (1988)	USA	358 (90% outpatients; 10% inpatients)	Specific assessment form using DSM-III criteria	73.5[l]
Jackson et al. (1991b)	Australia	112 (inpatients)	SIPD using DSM-III-R criteria	67[m]
Kass et al. (1985)	USA	609 (outpatients)	4-point rating format using DSM-III criteria	51[n]
Kastrup (1987)	Denmark	11 340 (inpatients)	Clinical assessment using ICD-8 criteria	(a) 18.3[o] (b) 16.7[o] (c) 15.2[p] (d) 15.7[p]
Kennedy et al. (1990)	Canada	44 (inpatients)[q]	MCMI and BSI, using DSM-III-R criteria	93[q]
Kroll et al. (1981)	USA	117 (inpatients)	DIB using DSM-III criteria	18[r]
Loranger (1990)	USA	(a) 5143 (b) 5771 (inpatients)	Clinical assessment using DSM-II criteria (a) and DSM-III criteria (b)	(a) 19.1 (b) 49.2
Loranger et al. (1991)	USA	84 (inpatients)	PDE using DSM-III criteria	(a) 58 (b) 50[s]
McGlashan (1986a)	USA	532 (inpatients)	Clinical assessment using DSM-III criteria	32[t]
Mezzich et al. (1982)	USA	1111 (inpatients and outpatients)	Initial evaluation form using DSM-III and ICD-9 criteria	21.4[u]
Mezzich et al. (1990)	USA	4141 (38% inpatients, 62% outpatients)[v]	Initial evaluation form using DSM-III and ICD-9 criteria	14.0[v]
Nace et al. (1991)	USA	100 (inpatients)[w]	SCID-II using DSM-III-R criteria	57
Nurnberg et al. (1991)	USA	100 (outpatients)[x]	Semistructured interview using DSM-III-R criteria	62
Nussbaum & Rogers (1992)	Canada	82 (inpatients)	SCID-PQ using DSM-III-R criteria	NA[y]
Oldham et al. (1992)	USA	100 (inpatients)	SCID-II using DSM-III-R criteria	NA[z]
Oldham & Skodol (1991)	USA	129 268 (inpatients and outpatients)[aa]	Clinical assessment using DSM-III and ICD-9 criteria	10.8[aa]

Table 8 (cont.)

Author(s)	Country	Size of sample	Method of assessment[a]	Prevalence (%)
Pfohl et al. (1986)	USA	131 (inpatients)	SIPD using DSM-III criteria	51[bb]
Pilgrim & Mann (1990)	United Kingdom	120 (inpatients)[cc]	SAP using ICD-10 criteria	36[cc]
Pilkonis & Frank (1988)	USA	119 (outpatients)[dd]	Hirschfeld-Klerman Personality Battery; PAS using DSM-III criteria	51[dd]
Reich (1987b)	USA	170 (outpatients)	SIPD (a), PDQ (b) and MCMI (c), using DSM-III criteria	(a) 48.8 (b) 60.0 (c) 66.7[ee]
Reich & Troughton (1988)	USA	(a) 88 (inpatients)[ff] (b) 82 (outpatients) (c) 40 (normal controls)	SIPD using DSM-III criteria ((a) and (b)); PDQ using DSM-III criteria ((c))	(a) 43 (b) 55 (c) 20
Ross et al. (1988)	Canada	501 (outpatients)[gg]	DIS using DSM-III criteria	47[gg]
Rounsaville et al. (1991)	USA	298 (inpatients and outpatients)[hh]	SADS using DSM-III-R criteria	7.7[hh]
Shea et al. (1990)	USA	239 (outpatients)[ii]	PAF using DSM-III criteria	74[ii]
Turner et al. (1991)	USA	68 (outpatients)[jj]	SCID-II using DSM-III-R criteria	37[jj]
Tyrer et al. (1983)	United Kingdom	316 (12 inpatients; 304 outpatients)[kk]	PAS using ICD-8 criteria	39.9[kk]
Zanarini et al. (1987)	USA	43 (inpatients)	DIPD using DSM-III criteria	81[ll]
Zimmerman et al. (1988)	USA	66 (inpatients)	SIPD with informant (a) or patient (b), using DSM-III criteria	(a) 58 (b) 36

[a] See page x.
[b] Patients receiving treatment for alcohol abuse.
[c] Among the patients surveyed, 97% had an axis I diagnosis and about half had an affective disorder.
[d] Patients with obsessive–compulsive PD. Mixed dependent and histrionic PDs were the most common; compulsive PD was found in only 6% of patients.
[e] Patients seen in a private psychiatric practice over a 5-year period.
[f] Patients discharged from a psychiatric facility over a 1-year period; 101 received a primary diagnosis of PD.
[g] Patients admitted with major psychiatric disorders. The prevalence of PDs among patients with depression, schizophrenia and manic disorder was 54%, 39% and 39%, respectively.
[h] Each patient had a mean of 4.5 diagnoses of PD. The most common diagnoses were borderline PD (in 62% of patients) and histrionic PD (in 61%).
[i] The most common diagnoses were affective disorder, antisocial PD and borderline PD. Patients with PDs were male, under 36 years of age and had problems in social functioning.
[j] Patients suffering from depression; among them, 36 (68%) met criteria for borderline PD.

I disorder (especially affective disorders) and a PD, it is not possible to reach any conclusion on the basis of the available studies, as the prevalence rates found are very different. These differences are related to differences in sampling, diagnostic criteria and assessment methods employed, coverage and accessibility of mental health services and a variety of other sociocultural factors. The rates are, however, more consistent in some of the studies carried out among treated patients. The most common PD seems to be borderline PD, followed by schizotypal and histrionic PDs. These three disorders are also characterized by severe impairments in social functioning and by the appearance of symptoms that require the patient's admission to hospital, such as suicidal behaviour, impulsive substance abuse and cognitive–perceptual abnormalities. In outpatient settings, dependent and passive–aggressive PDs are also common.

Footnotes to Table 8 (cont.)

[k] Samples made up of patients who were discharged consecutively from two psychiatric facilities; among them, 23.2% and 19.8% had borderline PD.

[l] Patients receiving treatment from 287 psychiatrists. The most common diagnoses were borderline PD (in 21%) and compulsive PD (in 11%).

[m] Among the sample, 21% had one PD and 46% had more than two PDs. An association was found between schizophrenia and antisocial and schizotypal PDs.

[n] The most common diagnosis was borderline PD (in 11%).

[o] Revolving-door patients, first diagnosis and last diagnosis.

[p] Non-revolving-door patients, first diagnosis and last diagnosis.

[q] Patients with eating disorders. Borderline, dependent and passive–aggressive PDs were most common.

[r] Refers to the prevalence of borderline PD.

[s] Sample made up of patients evaluated at entry (a) and at follow-up (b). Borderline, avoidant and dependent PDs were the most common PDs.

[t] Patients who met the DSM-III criteria or Gunderson's criteria for borderline PD.

[u] For 33 patients (3%), the principal diagnosis was the primary diagnosis in axis II.

[v] Among patients with a PD, approximately 7% were in cluster A, 45% in cluster B, 19% in cluster C and 30% in cluster D. Somatoform disorders and substance abuse were the most common axis I diagnoses (in 36% and 25% respectively).

[w] Sample comprised middle-class patients receiving treatment for substance abuse.

[x] Sample comprised patients with any minor axis I diagnosis. Avoidant (24%), borderline (20%) and histrionic PDs (17%) were most common.

[y] Borderline, paranoid and obsessive–compulsive PDs were most common.

[z] A total of 290 PDs were diagnosed. The most common diagnoses were borderline, avoidant and dependent PDs.

[aa] Sample included all patients who attended the New York State Office of Mental Health over a 1-year period. Among those with a PD, 17.2% had a diagnosis of borderline PD. Schizoaffective disorders, major affective disorders, dysthymia and substance abuse were more common among patients with PDs.

[bb] Histrionic (30%) and borderline PDs (29%) were the most common diagnoses; 54% had two or more PDs.

[cc] Sample comprised patients admitted for the first time over a 1-year period. Among patients with a PD, anxious and impulsive PDs were the most common diagnoses.

[dd] Patients receiving treatment for recurrent unipolar depression. The most common PDs were avoidant PD (30%) and compulsive PD (19%).

[ee] Among the sample, 45% were diagnosed as having a PD on two out of three assessment methods; the prevalence of histrionic PD was higher among females, while that of paranoid, compulsive and antisocial PDs was higher among males.

[ff] Patients suffering from panic disorder.

[gg] Patients seeking treatment for substance dependency; 47% had a diagnosis of antisocial PD.

[hh] Patients seeking treatment for cocaine abuse; 7.7% had a diagnosis of antisocial PD.

[ii] Patients with major depressive disorder included in the NIMH Treatment of Depression Collaborative Research Program. Among patients with PDs, 57% had a diagnosis of two or more PDs. Compulsive, avoidant, dependent and paranoid PD were the most frequent diagnoses.

[jj] Patients with social phobias. Over 75% of the patients received subthreshold ratings for one or more PDs. Avoidant and obsessive PD were the most common.

[kk] Patients with neurosis. Anankastic PD was the most common diagnosis.

[ll] Among patients with PDs, 34 (97%) had two or more PDs. Borderline PD was the most common diagnosis (26%).

In a study carried out among 2344 outpatients attending a public psychiatric facility and having a diagnosis of PD, made according to DSM-III criteria, the most common PDs were cluster B disorders and the least common were cluster A (Fabrega et al., 1991). A highly significant level of demographic variation or heterogeneity was also manifest across the various clusters.

In the only study carried out among patients attending a private psychiatric practice ($n=486$ outpatients), 39% were diagnosed as having a PD (Berger, 1985). Borderline (9.7%) and obsessive–compulsive PD (8.2%) were most common.

In some studies it has been possible to assess the long-term outcome of patients with a primary or a secondary diagnosis of PD. For instance, in the Chestnut Lodge Follow-up Study (McGlashan, 1986a), among all inpatients discharged between 1950 and 1975 and a smaller cohort of non-discharged inpatients from the same period ($n=532$), 169 patients (32%) either met the DSM-III criteria for borderline PD or met the criteria for the same disorder proposed by Gunderson et al. (1981); 52 patients (9.8%) met both criteria. The follow-up study was based on a smaller sample of 94 patients diagnosed as suffering only from borderline PD, with no other axis I disorder identified, the majority of whom were single females. Prior to their first contact with psychiatric services, they were likely to be at least moderately impaired in all adaptive areas (social and sexual). Onset was usually in late adolescence with progression of symptoms in the 20s. At follow-up, these patients were generally functioning well as regards their basic living situations, and they were also moderately active socially. Most of these patients showed evidence of psychopathology; they were generally comparable with unipolar patients and scored better than patients with schizophrenia on most indices of outcome. Outcome also varied with time, with borderline patients functioning best in the second decade after discharge. In the same study, McGlashan (1986b) found that 44% of the patients with schizotypal PD also received a diagnosis of schizophrenia; 25% of those with schizophrenia were also diagnosed as having schizotypal PD.

Some studies have investigated the hospital admission rate of patients with PDs over time and they allow us to assess the impact of diagnostic changes on the overall prevalence rate of patients with PDs in contact with psychiatric services.

Mors (1988) found that, in Denmark, sex- and age-standardized rates of first-time admissions of patients with borderline PD (as diagnosed according to ICD-8 criteria) significantly increased during 1970–85. There was no sex difference in the application of this diagnosis, but a generation effect, with the highest increases occurring in the age group 15–34 years. This increase was particularly marked in urban areas, and might be explained in terms of a change in diagnostic criteria. This hypothesis has received support from another analysis of data concerning admissions to psychiatric institutions in Denmark in the years 1975, 1980 and 1985; an increase in the prevalence of diagnosis of borderline PD among male inpatients (from 5% to 20% of the total sample) was found in parallel with a decrease in the prevalence of diagnosis of psychopathy (from 22% to 7%) (Simonsen & Mellergard, 1988). Therefore, the authors suggest that those who were previously diagnosed as suffering from psychopathy were subsequently diagnosed as having borderline PD. The shift, although visible, was less marked for women.

This same phenomenon, i.e. a change in diagnostic criteria as explanation for the increased rate of PDs among psychiatric patients, has been studied in a survey carried out in one of the largest university-affiliated psychiatric hospitals of the USA (Loranger, 1990). Comparing the diagnoses given to 10 914 inpatients admitted in the last 5 years before the introduction of DSM-III ($n=5143$) with those given in the first 5 years after the introduction of DSM-III ($n=5771$), a significant increase was found in the diagnosis of PDs, together with a significant decrease in the diagnosis of schizophrenia and a corresponding increase in the diagnosis of affective disorders. The percentage of patients with a diagnosis of PD rose from 19.1% to 49.2%. The most frequent diagnostic categories employed following the introduction of DSM-III were atypical, mixed or other PDs (33%) and borderline PD (27%).

Similarly, Blashfield et al. (1992) analysed the effects of the introduction of DSM-III-R. A sample of 73 inpatients and outpatients were assessed for DSM-III and DSM-III-R criteria using the SIPD and the revised version of the SIPD (SIPD-R) respectively. Significant increases in the rates of diagnosis of some PDs were found, which were most evident in the case of paranoid PD (from 3% to 22%), avoidant PD (from 13% to 33%) and obsessive–compulsive PD (from 15% to 28%); in contrast, the rate of diagnosis of schizotypal, borderline and dependent PDs decreased with the move from DSM-III to DSM-III-R. An analysis of the diagnostic criteria for each disorder demonstrated that small, apparently minor changes in the wording of the criteria may sometimes have major effects on the rate of diagnosis of PDs and on the type of diagnosis in individual patients. Kilbourne et al. (1991) carried out a survey of admissions to psychiatric institutes among active military personnel in the United States Navy during 1981–84. Among 27 210 inpatients admitted with a non-psychotic mental disorder as the primary diagnosis, 4581 (16.8%) had a primary diagnosis of PD.

National data from selected countries are also available concerning the prevalence of PDs among inpatients admitted to psychiatric hospitals. In England and Wales, 7.6% of all admissions and 8.5% of first admissions over a 1-year period were diagnosed as having PDs (Department of Health and Social Security, 1985), while in Scotland in 1986, 3.9% of all males and 4.4% of all females admitted had a diagnosis of PD (Information and Statistics Division, 1988).

In New Zealand, a survey was carried out of all inpatients admitted to psychiatric hospitals over a 7-year period with a primary diagnosis of PD (according to ICD-9 criteria) ($n=6447$) (Mulder, 1991). Despite a decrease in the total number of admissions, the prevalence rates for each PD remained consistent. The most common diagnostic category was unspecified PDs, which constituted 45% of the total sample; the next largest group was asthenic PD (12%). Patients with PDs were significantly younger and included a slightly higher proportion of women compared with patients with other psychiatric disorders. Furthermore, among the group with PDs, there were significant differences between men and women in marital status (two-thirds of the men and nearly half of the women had never been married) and admission status (more men than women had an involuntary admission).

In Ireland, the prevalence of diagnosis of PD among patients admitted to psychiatric hospitals in 1988 was 30.8 per 100 000 for all admissions and 9.4 per 100 000 for the first admissions (O'Connor & Walsh, 1991). The admission rate was similar for males (32.5 per 100 000) and females (29.1 per 100 000); the highest rate was in the age group 35–44 years and among unskilled manual workers. The large majority of the patients admitted with a diagnosis of PD had a hospital stay of less than one month.

In the USA, on a selected day in 1986, there were a total of 3893 inpatients in psychiatric facilities with a primary diagnosis of PD (equivalent to 2.4% of all psychiatric inpatients) (Shea et al., 1990). During 1986, there were 29 910 admissions with a primary diagnosis of PD (1.9% of all psychiatric admissions). The majority of patients with such a diagnosis had a hospital stay of 9 days. Among all people receiving outpatient psychiatric treatment on the same day, there were 81 731 (5.9% of the total) with a diagnosis of PD; during 1986, 136 903 people (6.4% of the total) were admitted as outpatients with the same diagnosis.

The epidemiological findings in treated samples are especially important, given that the presence of a PD among those suffering from an axis I disorder can be a major variable in predicting the natural history of the disorder and the outcome of treatment (Reich & Green, 1991).

Comorbidity of personality disorders

An important issue to be considered in the study of PDs is comorbidity. There are two types of comorbidity which need to be discussed: (i) comorbidity among personality disorders, and (ii) comorbidity with other psychiatric disorders.

Comorbidity among personality disorders

Several studies have shown a high rate of comorbidity among different PDs (Widiger & Rogers, 1989). Many patients who meet the criteria for one PD meet the criteria for another, and this phenomenon is especially common in inpatient settings. Some studies, which employed semistructured interviews for the diagnostic assessment of PDs, have found an average of four PDs per patient (Skodol et al., 1988; Widiger et al., 1986). While this phenomenon could reflect a low specificity of diagnostic criteria for some PDs, it might also reflect a tendency for certain PDs to coexist in the same person. So far, research on this specific topic has been limited; only a few studies have assessed the comorbidity rate among patients with a diagnosis of PD (Dahl, 1986; Morey, 1988; Pfohl et al., 1986).

The highest comorbidity rate appears to occur with borderline PD, with frequent coexistence of borderline and histrionic PDs. Borderline PD is also frequently found together with other PDs, including dissocial, schizotypal and dependent PDs. A recent review paper has suggested that the coexistence of borderline and schizotypal PDs might essentially reflect the different manifestations of personality psychopathology, which as such could commonly coexist in the same person (Kavoussi & Siever, 1992). Anxious PD frequently coexists with dependent and schizoid PDs, and also with histrionic and passive–aggressive PDs (as defined in DSM-III-R).

Further studies are needed to determine the effect of the comorbidity rate on the outcome of PDs.

Comorbidity with other psychiatric disorders

Another important aspect to be considered is the comorbidity between PDs and other psychiatric disorders. The assessment of such comorbidity can be especially difficult when the patient is suffering from the latter disorder at the time of the assessment, because this can affect the assessment of a PD.

Perhaps the most common and best studied comorbidity is between PDs and affective disorders. Many authors have stressed that among patients suffering from affective disorders there is a high comorbidity rate, particularly with regard to borderline PD, antisocial PD, avoidant PD and dependent PD (Alnaes & Torgersen, 1990; Klerman & Hirschfeld, 1988; Links et al., 1988). Studies of clinical populations have found very high rates of PDs among inpatients with major depressive disorder; among patients with unipolar depression, the prevalence rate of borderline PD was 23–67% (Docherty et al., 1986). Gunderson & Phillips (1991) have recently reviewed the relationship between borderline PD and depression. On the basis of evidence from family history, comorbidity, phenomenology, research and pathogenesis, the authors concluded that a surprisingly weak and nonspecific relationship exists between these disorders. However, they also pointed out that the available data, while giving most support to this hypothesis, do not rule out the possibility that the factors leading to depressive disorders and borderline PD could interact in some way.

In a recent study, 50 outpatients with bipolar affective disorder who were receiving long-term treatment with lithium were assessed with the PDQ (O'Connell et al., 1991). Twenty-nine (58%) of them scored for one or more PDs, with a mean of 1.42 diagnoses per patient. The majority of PD diagnoses were from cluster B, with borderline the most prevalent. Two studies have also found very similar personality traits between patients suffering from affective disorders and patients with panic disorder (Reich et al., 1987b; Reich & Troughton, 1988).

In the National Institute of Mental Health Treatment of Depression Collaborative Study, among 239 outpatients diagnosed as suffering from a major depressive disorder and assigned to one of four 16-week treatment schedules, 74% also received a diagnosis of PD (Shea et al., 1990). The most common disorder, found in 65% of patients, was in the anxious–fearful cluster

(cluster C). Patients with PDs had a worse outcome than patients without PDs; they were less likely to reach a clinical recovery and had significantly less improvement in social functioning, while they did not show any significant difference in terms of work functioning or in mean rating scores.

In the study by Fabrega et al. (1991), the rate of axis I comorbidity was highest among patients with a cluster C PD and lowest among those with a cluster A PD. Moreover, each PD cluster showed a specific pattern of axis I comorbidity: psychotic disorders were associated with cluster A, substance abuse with cluster B (which includes antisocial PD), and major depression and anxiety disorders with cluster C.

Other studies have also found an association between PDs and substance abuse (Reich & Thompson, 1987), alcohol abuse (Guze, 1976; Lewis et al., 1982, 1985) and somatoform disorders (Koenigsberg et al., 1985). A survey of the medical records of psychiatric inpatients discharged from general hospitals in the USA in 1980 showed that, in a total sample of 92 509 patients who had, at the time of discharge, a diagnosis of both mental disorder and substance abuse, 19% had a diagnosis of PD (Kiesler et al., 1991). However, the prevalence of PDs in this population may have been higher, since American clinicians often used to include only the primary diagnosis in discharge summary records.

As regards the comorbidity between substance abuse and borderline PD, it should be noted that substance abuse has been included as one of the diagnostic criteria for borderline PD in DSM-III (but not in ICD-10). High rates of substance abuse have been found among patients with borderline PD by Andrulonis et al. (1982) (69%), Dulit et al. (1990) (67%) and Akiskal et al. (1985) (55%), although Baxter et al. (1984) and Frances et al. (1984) have reported lower rates (11% and 23% respectively).

It is also acknowledged that personality disorders can be common among patients manifesting suicidal or parasuicidal behaviour. In the Iowa record-linkage study in the USA, an investigation of 5412 formerly hospitalized psychiatric patients found that 68 had committed suicide and 38 had died from accidental causes (Black et al., 1985). Both the suicide rate among men with PDs and the accidental death rate among men and women with PDs were significantly higher than the rates found in the general population. In Sweden, a study of a cohort of 50 465 men conscripted for military service in 1969–70 found that a diagnosis of PD at conscription was associated with a significantly increased risk for future suicide (Allebeck & Allgulander, 1990). A nationwide study of autopsies carried out in Finland (Marttunen et al., 1991) on adolescents ($n = 53$) who committed suicide over a 1-year period (1987–88) found that 17 (32%) had been diagnosed as having a PD.

With regard to specific PDs, in a study of 500 randomly selected psychiatric outpatients, followed up for a mean of 7 years, both the suicide rate and the accidental death rate were significantly higher among patients with antisocial PD than among patients with other disorders (Martin et al., 1985). In the case of borderline PD, suicidal behaviour is included in both ICD-10 and DSM-III diagnostic criteria for this disorder. However, in the few empirical studies carried out to document the frequency of suicidal behaviour among patients with borderline PD, rather lower rates of completed suicides have been found: Akiskal et al. (1985) reported a rate of 4% during a 6–36-month follow-up, while Stone et al. (1987) found a rate of 9.5% on 15–20-year follow-up. In another retrospective study carried out in Sweden of 134 psychiatric patients who committed suicide between 1961 and 1980 in a selected catchment area of 250 000 inhabitants, there was a progressive increase in the suicide rate among patients with borderline PD over the period of study; however, the overall prevalence of borderline PD in the sample was only 12% (Kullgren et al., 1986). In contrast, a study carried out among 58 adolescents and young adults (aged 15–29 years), who committed suicide between 1984 and 1987, found that 19 (33%) had been diagnosed as having borderline PD (Runeson & Beskow, 1991).

Very high prevalence rates of parasuicidal behaviour (48–65%) have been reported among patients with borderline PD by Fyer et al. (1988b), Ovenstone (1973) and Philips (1970). In another study carried out among 53 individuals attending an emergency psychiatric service and complaining of specific suicidal ideation (but without any suicidal behaviour), 21 (40%) were diagnosed as suffering from a PD according to ICD-9 criteria (Hawley et al., 1991).

Studies carried out in other institutions

In other institutional settings, such as prisons, several studies have shown that the prevalence rate of antisocial PD can be as high as 75%. Two recent studies carried out among prisoners using DSM-III criteria have found prevalence rates of 57% ($n = 180$) (Bland et al., 1990) and 39% ($n = 246$) (Hare, 1983). In the study by Bland et al. (1990), the prevalence rate was seven times that found in a comparative study carried out among the local general population.

Other studies have found lower prevalence rates for all PDs. In a recent population survey carried out in the United Kingdom and based on a 5% sample of men serving prison sentences ($n = 404$ young offenders and 1365 adult men), to whom a semistructured interview was given, 10% of the inmates were diagnosed as suffering from a PD according to ICD-9 criteria (Gunn et al., 1991). This rate is similar to the rates of 13% and 8% found in other prison surveys using clinical criteria (Roger, 1950), although it is considerably lower than the rate of 22% found in a previous British survey (Gunn et al., 1978). It again seems likely that the diagnostic criteria and the assessment methods employed have affected the rates found in different studies.

3.3 Temporal trends in the prevalence of personality disorders

Few studies provide information about temporal trends in the prevalence of PDs. The main evidence comes from two studies of the general population, which are briefly reviewed below.

In a 15-year follow-up survey of three communities in Taiwan, China, age-specific prevalence rates of PDs of 1.0 per thousand and 1.4 per thousand were found respectively in 1946–48 and 1961–63, using an unstructured psychiatric interview (Lin et al., 1989). The difference in rates between the two periods of observation and between the two sexes was not significant. It should be noted that the prevalence rates of PDs found in this study are among the lowest ever recorded, and raise important questions regarding the factors responsible.

In the Upper Bavarian studies, 1536 people were first assessed in 1975–79 using the Goldberg interview; 18.6% of them were suffering from a significant mental disorder in the 7 days prior to the interview and 0.7% (0.6% of males and 0.8% of females) were suffering from a PD (Dilling et al., 1989). From this sample, 1385 were interviewed again 5 years later; among them, 2.8% were suffering from a PD, with a significant increase in the prevalence rate compared with the previous investigation.

Therefore, while in Taiwan, China there was no increase in the prevalence of PDs over a 15-year period, in Germany a significant increase was found over the period of the study. However, it should be noted that neither of these studies was aimed at assessing the prevalence of PDs; the assessment methods employed cast many doubts about the reliability of the findings concerning PDs. As mentioned earlier, two other studies (Loranger, 1990; Mors, 1988) also showed a marked increase in the diagnosis of PDs in psychiatric inpatients over 10 years and 15 years respectively; however, the increase seems to be due to a change in the diagnostic criteria used rather than a true increase in the prevalence of PDs. In conclusion, further studies are needed to evaluate temporal trends in the prevalence of PDs.

4

Conclusions and recommendations for future studies

As mentioned at the beginning of this review, the epidemiology of PDs has not received as much attention as the epidemiology of other major psychiatric disorders. Nevertheless, the situation is starting to change and specific data are now available concerning the epidemiology of PDs in the community, in primary health care facilities, in psychiatric settings and in other institutions. However, as regards the epidemiology of PDs in the community, reliable data come essentially from three studies (Maier et al., 1992; Reich et al., 1989a; Zimmerman & Coryell, 1990), involving a total of about 1300 people from two countries (Germany and the USA). In addition, while there are excellent national and cross-national epidemiological data on dissocial PD, based on the same diagnostic methods, there are almost no data on other PDs from countries other than Germany and the USA. The lack of studies from developing countries is of particular concern. The results from the few studies carried out in China, Costa Rica, India, the Islamic Republic of Iran and Peru, indicate that the prevalence of PDs in developing countries may be significantly lower than in developed countries. Further studies on this issue would allow an understanding of the specific influence that sociocultural factors have in preventing the development of these disorders or in ameliorating their course.

In the epidemiological study of PDs, an important methodological problem is that, as shown in the studies reviewed above, some PDs have a very low prevalence rate; consequently epidemiological surveys carried out among the general population may require very large samples in order to identify a satisfactory number of cases, especially of the most rare types of specific PDs, and study their sociodemographic characteristics and the association of the PDs with other psychiatric disorders.

Another problem that will require further investigation is comorbidity in PDs. Several studies, carried out both in the community and in treated samples, have shown that individuals tend to manifest more than one PD. There seems to be a high comorbidity between certain PDs, including borderline, antisocial, schizotypal and avoidant PDs. In addition, the relationship between PDs and other psychiatric disorders will need to be carefully studied in view of the important implications that it might have for both clinical treatment and research. It has already been stressed that the presence of a PD can strongly affect the outcome of other psychiatric disorders. It will therefore be important to clarify, through longitudinal studies, the boundaries between the various disorders.

Many of the PDs are at an early stage of construct validation. Accordingly, further research should probably follow the general recommendations for validating a psychiatric disorder, including the need to differentiate the disorder from other disorders. Given the overlap of the PDs, this will be a challenging task. Furthermore, Livesley & Jackson (1992) have recently emphasized the need for ensuring the content validity of diagnostic concepts, defined by Kendell (1975) as the "demonstration that the defining character-istics of a given disorder are indeed inquired into and elicited before that diagnosis is made."

Another criterion is external validation. There are a number of possible psychological tests and behavioural indicators that could be used in validating PDs. Alternatively, biological markers could be employed; exploration of these will be important in future research.

In addition, studies are required to determine how the course or natural history of PDs may allow their differentiation. Few such studies have been carried out, largely because of the cost of prospective designs. However, prospective longitudinal studies can provide important scientific and clinical information that are simply not available from cross-sectional studies. This information would help to identify predictors of future PDs, modifying vari-ables, and medical and social service needs for patients and to determine the effect of temperament on the development of PDs. Temperament has been shown to be stable and could conceivably be an important predictive variable. Another issue that could be explored in such studies is the temporal consistency of PDs. Although PDs are, according to ICD-10 and DSM-III, long-lasting disorders, very limited data are available on their stability over time. For this reason it would be useful to investigate the epidemiology of PDs in different age groups, as well as the course of PDs. Longitudinal studies will also provide the main evidence for validating a PD (Rutter, 1987).

There is some indication that certain PDs (e.g. schizotypal, dissocial and anxious/avoidant PDs) may have genetic predisposing factors. It is now apparent that normal personality traits are heritable (McGuffin & Thapar, 1992). Future research should attempt to define the relationship between PDs and other psychiatric disorders. If some PDs are confirmed to be heritable, then it provides an opening for genetic mapping to identify populations at risk. Risk factors also need to be investigated.

Finally, treatment response is another important criterion for validating a disorder. Although PDs are considered stable and long-lasting, it is likely that effective treatments will ultimately be developed for the various PDs. In that case, treatment response will also be used to validate different types of PD.

References

Akhtar S, Byrne JP, Doghramji K (1986) The demographic profile of borderline personality disorder. *Journal of clinical psychiatry*, 47: 196–198.

Akiskal HS et al. (1985) Borderline: an adjective in search of a noun. *Journal of clinical psychiatry*, 46: 41–48.

Allan CA (1991) Psychological symptoms, psychiatric disorder and alcohol dependence amongst men and women attending a community-based voluntary agency and an alcohol treatment unit. *British journal of addiction*, 86: 419–427.

Allebeck P, Allgulander C (1990) Psychiatric diagnoses as predictors of suicide. *British journal of psychiatry*, 157: 339–344.

Allebeck P, Allgulander C, Fisher LD (1988) Predictors of completed suicide in a cohort of 50,465 young men: role of personality and deviant behaviour. *British medical journal*, 297: 176–178.

Allport GW (1937) *Personality: a psychological interpretation*. New York, Holt.

Alnaes R, Torgersen S (1988a) The relationship between DSM-III symptom disorders (axis I) and personality disorders (axis II) in an outpatient population. *Acta psychiatrica Scandinavica*, 78: 485–492.

Alnaes R, Torgersen S (1988b) DSM-III symptom disorders (axis I) and personality disorders (axis II) in an outpatient population. *Acta psychiatrica Scandinavica*, 78: 348–355.

Alnaes R, Torgersen S (1990) DSM-III personality disorders among patients with major depression, anxiety disorders, and mixed conditions. *Journal of nervous and mental disease*, 178: 693–698.

American Psychiatric Association (1980) *Diagnostic and statistical manual of mental disorders*, 3rd ed. Washington, DC, American Psychiatric Press.

American Psychiatric Association (1987) *Diagnostic and statistical manual of mental disorders*, 3rd ed., rev. Washington, DC, American Psychiatric Press.

American Psychiatric Association (in press) *Diagnostic and statistical manual of mental disorders*, 4th ed. Washington, DC, American Psychiatric Press.

Andreoli A et al. (1989) Personality disorders as a predictor of outcome. *Journal of personality disorders*, 3: 307–320.

Andrulonis PA et al. (1982) Borderline personality subcategories. *Journal of nervous and mental disease*, 170: 670–679.

Baer L et al. (1990) Standardized assessment of personality disorders in obsessive–compulsive disorder. *Archives of general psychiatry*, 47: 826–830.

Baron M (1981) *Schedule for Interviewing Borderlines*. New York, New York State Psychiatric Institute.

Baron M et al. (1985) A family study of schizophrenic and normal control probands: implications for the spectrum concept of schizophrenia. *American journal of psychiatry*, 142: 447–455.

Bash KW, Bash-Liechti J (1987) *Developing psychiatry*. Berlin, Springer-Verlag.

Baxter L et al. (1984) Dexamethasone suppression test and axis I diagnoses of inpatients with DSM-III borderline personality disorder. *Journal of clinical psychiatry*, 45: 150–153.

Berger J (1985) Private practice: the first five years. *Canadian journal of psychiatry*, 30: 566–571.

Birtchnell J (1988) Defining dependence. *British journal of medical psychology*, 61: 111–123.

Black DW, Warrack G, Winokur G (1985) The Iowa record-linkage study. *Archives of general psychiatry*, 42: 71–73.

Blackburn R (1988) On moral judgements and personality disorders. The myth of psychopathic personality. *British journal of psychiatry*, 153: 505–512.

Bland RC et al. (1990) Prevalence of psychiatric disorders and suicide attempts in a prison population. *Canadian journal of psychiatry*, 35: 407–413.

Bland RC, Newman SC, Orn H (1988a) Age of onset of psychiatric disorders. *Acta psychiatrica Scandinavica*, 77 (Suppl. 338): 43–49.

Bland RC, Orn H, Newman SC (1988b) Lifetime prevalence of psychiatric disorders in Edmonton. *Acta psychiatrica Scandinavica*, 77 (Suppl. 338): 24–32.

Blashfield RK (1991) An American view of the ICD-10 personality disorders. *Acta psychiatrica Scandinavica*, 82: 250–256.

Blashfield RK, Blum N, Pfohl B (1992) The effects of changing axis II diagnostic criteria. *Comprehensive psychiatry*, 33: 245–252.

Bremer J (1951) A social psychiatric investigation of a small community in northern Norway. *Acta psychiatrica et neurologica Scandinavica*, Suppl. 62.

Casey PR (1988) Epidemiology of personality disorders. In: Tyrer P, ed. *Personality disorders: diagnosis, management and course*. London, Wright.

Casey PR, Dillon S, Tyrer P (1984) The diagnostic status of patients with conspicuous psychiatric morbidity in primary care. *Psychological medicine*, 14: 673–681.

Casey PR, Tyrer PJ (1986) Personality, functioning and symptomatology. *Journal of psychiatric research*, 20: 363–374.

Castaneda R, Franco H (1985) Sex and ethnic distribution of borderline personality disorder in an inpatient sample. *American journal of psychiatry*, 142: 1202–1203.

Charney DS, Nelson JC, Quinlan DM (1981) Personality traits and disorder in depression. *American journal of psychiatry*, 138: 1601–1604.

Chen C et al. (1993) The Shatin Community Mental Health Survey in Hong Kong. II. Major findings. *Archives of general psychiatry*, 50: 125–133.

Cheung P (1991) Adult psychiatric epidemiology in China in the 80s. *Culture, medicine and psychiatry*, 15: 479–496.

Clark LA (1989) *The basic traits of PD: primary and higher-order dimensions.* Paper presented at the ninety-seventh convention of the American Psychological Association (unpublished document; available on request from the Division of Mental Health, World Health Organization, 1211 Geneva 27, Switzerland).

Cloninger CR (1987) *Tridimensional Personality Questionnaire (TPQ).* Washington, DC, Washington University School of Medicine, Department of Psychiatry and Genetics.

Conte H et al. (1980) A self-report borderline scale: discriminative validity and preliminary norms. *Journal of nervous and mental disease*, 168: 428–435.

Cooper B (1965) A study of one hundred chronic psychiatric patients identified in general practice. *British journal of psychiatry*, 111: 595–605.

Cooper B (1972) Clinical and social aspects of chronic neurosis. *Proceedings of the Royal Society of Medicine*, 65: 512–519.

Cutting J et al. (1986) Personality and psychosis: use of the standardized assessment of personality. *Acta psychiatrica Scandinavica*, 73: 87–92.

Dahl AA (1986) Some aspects of DSM-III personality disorders illustrated by a consecutive sample of hospitalized patients. *Acta psychiatrica Scandinavica*, 73 (Suppl. 328): 61–66.

Department of Health and Social Security (1985) *Mental illness hospitals and units in England. Results from the Mental Health Inquiry.* Statistical Bulletin. Government Statistical Service. London, HMSO.

Dilling H, Weyerer S, Fichter M (1989) The Upper Bavarian studies. *Acta psychiatrica Scandinavica*, 79 (Suppl. 348): 113–140.

Docherty JP, Fiester SJ, Shea T (1986) Syndrome diagnosis and personality disorder. In: Frances AJ, Hales RE, eds. *APA annual review, Vol. 5.* Washington, DC, American Psychiatric Press, pp. 315–355.

Dodwell D (1988) Comparison of self-ratings with informant-ratings of pre-morbid personality on two personality rating scales. *Psychological medicine*, 18: 495–502.

Dowson JH, Berrios GE (1991) Factor structure of DSM-III-R personality disorders shown by self-report questionnaire: implications for classifying and assessing personality disorders. *Acta psychiatrica Scandinavica*, 84: 555–560.

Dulit RA et al. (1990) Substance use in borderline personality disorder. *American journal of psychiatry*, 147: 1002–1007.

Endicott J, Spitzer RL (1978) A diagnostic interview: the Schedule for Affective Disorders and Schizophrenia. *Archives of general psychiatry*, 35: 837–844.

Essen-Moller E (1956) Individual traits and morbidity in a Swedish rural population. *Acta psychiatrica et neurologica Scandinavica*, Suppl. 100.

Fabrega H, Jr et al. (1991) On the homogeneity of personality disorder clusters. *Comprehensive psychiatry*, 32: 373–385.

Fabrega H, Jr et al. (1993) Personality disorders diagnosed at intake at a public psychiatric facility. *Hospital and community psychiatry*, 44: 159–162.

Frances A et al. (1984) Reliability of criteria for borderline personality disorder: a comparison of DSM-III and the Diagnostic Interview for Borderline Patients. *American journal of psychiatry*, 141: 1080–1084.

Friedman RC et al. (1983) History of suicidal behavior in depressed borderline inpatients. *American journal of psychiatry*, 140: 1023–1026.

Fyer MR et al. (1988a) Comorbidity of borderline personality disorder. *Archives of general psychiatry*, 45: 348–352.

Fyer MR et al. (1988b) Suicide attempts in patients with borderline personality disorder. *American journal of psychiatry*, 145: 737–739.

Gorton G, Akhtar S (1990) The literature on personality disorders, 1985–88: trends, issues and controversies. *Hospital and community psychiatry*, 41: 39–51.

Gunderson JG, Kolb J, Austin V (1981) The Diagnostic Interview for Borderline Patients. *American journal of psychiatry*, 138: 896–903.

Gunderson JG, Phillips KA (1991) A current view of the interface between borderline personality disorder and depression. *American journal of psychiatry*, 148: 967–975.

Gunderson JG, Ronningstam E, Bodkin A (1990) The Diagnostic Interview for Narcissistic Patients. *Archives of general psychiatry*, 47: 676–680.

Gunn J et al. (1978) *Psychiatric aspects of imprisonment*. London, Academic Press.

Gunn J, Maden A, Swinton M (1991) Treatment needs of prisoners with psychiatric disorders. *British medical journal*, 303: 338–341.

Guze SB (1976) *Criminality and psychiatric disorders*. New York, Oxford University Press.

Hare RD (1983) Diagnosis of antisocial personality disorder in two prison populations. *American journal of psychiatry*, 140: 887–890.

Hare RD, Hart SD, Harpur TJ (1991) Psychopathy and the DSM-IV criteria for antisocial personality disorder. *Journal of abnormal psychology*, 100: 391–398.

Hawley CJ et al. (1991) Suicidal ideation as a presenting complaint: associated diagnoses and characteristics in a casualty population. *British journal of psychiatry*, 159: 232–238.

Helgason T (1981) Psychiatric epidemiological studies in Iceland. In: Schulsinger F, Mednick SA, Knop J, eds. *Longitudinal research: methods and uses in behavioural sciences.* Boston, Marinus Nijoff, pp. 216–232.

Helgason T, Magnusson H (1989) The first 80 years of life: a psychiatric epidemiological study. *Acta psychiatrica Scandinavica*, 79 (Suppl. 348): 85–94.

Hwu HG, Yeh EK, Chang LY (1989) Prevalence of psychiatric disorders in Taiwan defined by the Chinese Diagnostic Interview Schedule. *Acta psychiatrica Scandinavica*, 79: 136–147.

Hyler SE et al. (1989) A comparison of clinical and self-report diagnoses of DSM-III personality disorders in 522 patients. *Comprehensive psychiatry*, 30: 170–178.

Hyler SE, Lyons M (1988) Factor analysis of the DSM-III personality disorder clusters: a replication. *Comprehensive psychiatry*, 29: 304–308.

Hyler SE, Reider RO (1984) *Personality Diagnostic Questionnaire, Revised (PDQR)*. New York, New York State Psychiatric Institute.

Information and Statistics Division (1988) *Scottish health statistics*. Edinburgh.

Jackson HJ et al. (1991a) Concordance between two personality disorder instruments with psychiatric inpatients. *Comprehensive psychiatry*, 32: 252–260.

Jackson HJ et al. (1991b) Diagnosing personality disorders in psychiatric inpatients. *Acta psychiatrica Scandinavica*, 83: 206–213.

Kass F et al. (1985) Scaled ratings of DSM-III personality disorders. *American journal of psychiatry*, 142: 627–630.

Kastrup M (1987) Who became revolving-door patients? Findings from a nation-wide cohort of first-time admitted psychiatric patients. *Acta psychiatrica Scandinavica*, 76: 80–88.

Kato M (1988) Issues on diagnosing and classifying personality disorders. In: Mezzich JE, von Cranach M, eds. *International Classification in Psychiatry*. Cambridge, Cambridge University Press, pp. 166–172.

Kavoussi RJ, Siever LJ (1992) Overlap between borderline and schizotypal personality disorders. *Comprehensive psychiatry*, 33: 7–12.

Kendell RE (1975) *The role of diagnosis in psychiatry*. Oxford, Blackwells.

Kennedy SH, McVey G, Katz R (1990) Personality disorders in anorexia nervosa and bulimia nervosa. *Journal of psychiatric research*, 24: 259–269.

Kessel N (1960) Psychiatric morbidity in a London general practice. *British journal of preventive and social medicine*, 14: 16–22.

Kiesler CA, Simpkins CG, Morton TL (1991) Prevalence of dual diagnoses of mental and substance abuse disorders in general hospitals. *Hospital and community psychiatry*, 42: 400–403.

Kilbourne B, Goodman J, Hilton S (1991) Predicting personality disorder diagnoses of hospitalized navy personnel. *Military medicine*, 156: 354–357.

Kinzie JD et al. (1992) Psychiatric epidemiology of an Indian village: a 19-year replication study. *Journal of nervous and mental disease*, 180: 33–39.

Klein M (1985) *Wisconsin Personality Inventory (WISPI)*. Madison, WI, University of Wisconsin, Department of Psychiatry.

Klerman GL, Hirschfeld RMA (1988) Personality as a vulnerability factor: with special attention to clinical depression. In: Henderson AS, Burrows GD, eds. *Handbook of social psychiatry*. Amsterdam, Elsevier, pp. 41–53.

Koegel P (1988) The prevalence of specific psychiatric disorders among homeless individuals in the inner city of Los Angeles. *Archives of general psychiatry*, 45: 1085–1092.

Koenigsberg HW et al. (1985) The relationship between syndrome and personality disorder in DSM-III: experience with 2462 patients. *American journal of psychiatry*, 142: 207–213.

Kraepelin E (1921) *Manic depressive insanity and paranoia* (translated by R.M. Barclay from the 8th edition of *Lehrbuch der Psychiatrie*. [*Textbook of psychiatry*.] Vols III and IV). Edinburgh, Livingstone.

Kroll J et al. (1981) Borderline personality disorder: construct validity of the concept. *Archives of general psychiatry*, 38: 1021–1026.

Kullgren G, Renberg E, Jacobsson L (1986) An empirical study of borderline personality disorder and psychiatric suicides. *Journal of nervous and mental disease*, 174: 328–331.

Langner TS, Michael ST (1963) *Life stress and mental health. The Midtown Manhattan Study*. London, Collier, MacMillan.

Lee CK et al. (1990) Psychiatric epidemiology in Korea, part I: gender and age differences in Seoul. *Journal of nervous and mental disease*, 178: 242–252.

Leighton AH (1959) *My name is Legion: the Stirling County Study of Psychiatric Disorder and Sociocultural Environment*. New York, Basic Books.

Leonhard K (1959) *Aufteilung der endogenen Psychosen*. [Distribution of endogenous psychoses.] Berlin, Akademie Verlag.

Levav I et al. (1989) Salud mental para todos en América Latine y el Caribe. Bases epidemiológicas para le acción. [Mental health for all in Latin America and the Caribbean. Epidemiological bases for action.] *Bolétin de la Oficina Sanitaria Panamericana*, 107: 196–219.

Lewis A (1974) Psychopathic personality: a most elusive category. *Psychological medicine*, 4: 133–140.

Lewis CE et al. (1982) Psychiatric diagnostic predispositions to alcoholism. *Comprehensive psychiatry*, 23: 451–461.

Lewis CE, Robins L, Rice J (1985) Association of alcoholism with antisocial personality disorder in urban men. *Journal of nervous and mental disease*, 173: 166–170.

Lin TY et al. (1989) Effects of social change on mental disorders in Taiwan: observations based on a 15-year follow-up survey of general populations in three communities. *Acta psychiatrica Scandinavica*, 79 (Suppl. 348): 11–34.

Links PS et al. (1988) Characteristics of borderline personality disorder: a Canadian study. *Canadian journal of psychiatry*, 33: 336–340.

Livesley WJ, Jackson DN (1992) Guidelines for developing, evaluating and revising the classification of personality disorders. *Journal of nervous and mental disease*, 180: 609–618.

Loranger AW (1990) The impact of DSM-III on diagnostic practice in a university hospital. *Archives of general psychiatry*, 47: 672–675.

Loranger AW et al. (1991) The WHO/ADAMHA International Pilot Study of Personality Disorders: background and purpose. *Journal of personality disorders*, 5: 296–306.

Maier W et al. (1992) Prevalences of personality disorders (DSM-III-R) in the community. *Journal of personality disorders*, 6: 187–196.

Mann AH, Jenkins R, Belsey E (1981) The twelve-month outcome of patients with neurotic illness in general practice. *Psychological medicine*, 11: 535–550.

Martin RL et al. (1985) Mortality in a follow-up of 500 psychiatric outpatients. *Archives of general psychiatry*, 42: 58–61.

Marttunen MJ et al. (1991) Mental disorders in adolescent suicide. *Archives of general psychiatry*, 48: 834.

McGlashan TH (1986a) The Chestnut Lodge follow-up study: III. Long-term outcome of borderline personalities. *Archives of general psychiatry*, 43: 20–30.

McGlashan TH (1986b) Schizotypal personality disorder Chestnut Lodge follow-up study: VI. Long-term follow-up perspectives. *Archives of general psychiatry*, 43: 329–334.

McGuffin P, Thapar A (1992) The genetics of personality disorder. *British journal of psychiatry*, 160: 12–23.

Merikangas KR (1989) Epidemiology of DSM-III personality disorders. In: Michels R et al., eds. *Psychiatry*, Vol. 3. Philadelphia, Lippincott, pp. 1–16.

Merikangas KR, Weissman MM (1986) Epidemiology of DSM-III axis II personality disorders. In: Frances AJ, Hales RE, eds. *APA annual review*, Vol. 5. Washington, DC, American Psychiatric Press, pp. 258–278.

Mezzich JE, Coffman GA, Goodpastor SM (1982) A format for DSM-III diagnostic formulation: experience with 1111 consecutive patients. *American journal of psychiatry*, 139: 591–596.

Mezzich JE et al. (1990) Patterns of psychiatric comorbidity in a large population presenting for care. In: Maser JD, Cloninger CR, eds. *Comorbidity of mood and anxiety disorders*. Washington, DC, American Psychiatric Press, pp. 189–204.

Millon T (1982) *Millon clinical multiaxial inventory manual*, 2nd ed. Minnetonka, MN, National Computer Systems.

Morey LC (1988) Personality disorders in DSM-III and DSM-III-R: convergence, coverage and internal consistency. *American journal of psychiatry*, 145: 573–577.

Mors O (1988) Increasing incidence of borderline states in Denmark from 1970–1985. *Acta psychiatrica Scandinavica*, 77: 575–583.

Mulder RT (1991) Personality disorders in New Zealand hospitals. *Acta psychiatrica Scandinavica*, 84: 197–202.

Nace EP, Davis CW, Gaspari J (1991) Axis II comorbidity in substance abusers. *American journal of psychiatry*, 148: 118–120.

Nestadt G et al. (1990) An epidemiological study of histrionic personality disorder. *Psychological medicine*, 20: 413–422.

Nestadt G et al. (1991) DSM-III compulsive personality disorder: an epidemiological survey. *Psychological medicine*, 21: 461–471.

Neugebauer R, Dohrenwend BP, Dohrenwend BS (1980) Formulation of hypotheses about the true prevalence of functional psychiatric disorders among adults in the U.S. In: Dohrenwend BP et al., eds. *Mental illness in the United States: epidemiological estimates*. New York, Praeger, pp. 56–92.

Nurnberg GH et al. (1991) The comorbidity of borderline personality disorder and other DSM-III-R axis II personality disorders. *American journal of psychiatry*, 148: 1371–1377.

Nussbaum D, Rogers R (1992) Screening psychiatric patients for axis II disorders. *Canadian journal of psychiatry*, 37: 658–660.

O'Connell RA, Mayo JA, Sciutto MS (1991) PDQ-R personality disorders in bipolar patients. *Journal of affective disorders*, 23: 217–221.

O'Connor A, Walsh D (1991) *Activities of Irish psychiatric hospitals and units 1988*. Dublin, Health Research Board.

Oldham JM et al. (1992) Diagnosis of DSM-III-R personality disorders by two structured interviews: patterns of comorbidity. *American journal of psychiatry*, 149: 213–220.

Oldham JM, Skodol AE (1991) Personality disorders in the public sector. *Hospital and community psychiatry*, 42: 481–487.

Ovenstone IK (1973) Spectrum of suicidal behaviours in Edinburgh. *British journal of preventive and social medicine*, 27: 27–35.

Perry JC (1982) *The Borderline Personality Disorder Scale (BPD-scale)*. Cambridge, MA, Cambridge Hospital.

Perry JC (1992) Problems and considerations in the valid assessment of personality disorders. *American journal of psychiatry*, 149: 1645–1653.

Perry JC, Vaillant GE (1989) Personality disorders. In: Kaghan HI, Sadock BJ, eds. *Comprehensive textbook of psychiatry*. Baltimore, William & Wirekins, pp. 1352–1386.

Pfohl B et al. (1986) DSM-III personality disorders: diagnostic overlap and inter-consistency of individual DSM-III criteria. *Comprehensive psychiatry*, 27: 21–34.

Pfohl B, Stangl D, Zimmerman M (1983) *Structured interview for DSM-III Personality Disorders (SIPD)*. Iowa, University of Iowa.

Philips AE (1970) Traits, attitudes and symptoms in a group of attempted suicides. *British journal of psychiatry*, 116: 475–482.

Pilgrim J, Mann A (1990) Use of the ICD-10 version of the Standardized Assessment of Personality to determine the prevalence of personality disorder in psychiatric in-patients. *Psychological medicine*, 20: 985–992.

Pilkonis PA, Frank E (1988) Personality pathology in recurrent depression: nature, prevalence, and relationship to treatment response. *American journal of psychiatry*, 145: 435–441.

Pincus HA et al. (1992) DSM-IV and new diagnostic categories: holding the line on proliferation. *American journal of psychiatry*, 149: 112–116.

Regier DA et al. (1990) Comorbidity of mental disorders with alcohol and other drug abuse. *Journal of the American Medical Association*, 264: 2511–2518.

Reich JH (1987a) Instruments measuring DSM-III and DSM-III-R personality disorders. *Journal of personality disorders*, 1: 220–240.

Reich JH (1987b) Sex distribution of DSM-III personality disorders in psychiatric outpatients. *American journal of psychiatry*, 144: 485–488.

Reich JH (1988) A family history method for DSM-III anxiety and personality disorders. *Psychiatry research*, 26: 131–139.

Reich JH (1989) Update on instruments to measure DSM-III and DSM-III-R personality disorders. *Journal of nervous and mental disease*, 177: 366–370.

Reich JH et al. (1987b) State and personality in depressed and panic patients. *American journal of psychiatry*, 144: 181–187.

Reich JH et al. (1989b) Utilization of medical resources in persons with DSM-III personality disorders in a community sample. *International journal of psychiatry in medicine*, 19: 1–9.

Reich JH, Green AI (1991) Effect of personality disorders on outcome of treatment. *Journal of nervous and mental disease*, 179: 74–82.

Reich JH, Nduaguba M, Yates W (1988) Age and sex distribution of DSM-III personality cluster traits in a community population. *Comprehensive psychiatry*, 29: 298–303.

Reich JH, Noyes R, Troughton E (1987a) Lack of agreement between instruments assessing DSM-III personality disorders. In: Millon T, ed. *Conference on the Millon Clinical Inventories, March 8 1987, Miami*. Minnetonka, MN, National Computer Systems.

Reich JH, Thompson WD (1987) Differential assortment of DSM-III personality disorder clusters in three populations. *British journal of psychiatry*, 150: 471–475.

Reich JH, Troughton E (1988) Frequency of DSM-III personality disorders in patients with panic disorder: comparison with psychiatric and normal control subjects. *Psychiatry research*, 26: 89–100.

Reich JH, Yates W, Nduaguba M (1989a) Prevalence of DSM-III personality disorders in the community. *Social psychiatry*, 24: 12–16.

Richman JA, Flaherty JA (1987) *Narcissistic Trait Scale (NTS)*. Chicago, University of Illinois, Department of Psychiatry.

Robins LN et al. (1981) National Institute of Mental Health Diagnostic Interview Schedule: its history, characteristics, and validity. *Archives of general psychiatry*, 39: 381–389.

Robins LN, Regier DA (1991) *Psychiatric disorders in America. The ECA Study*. New York, Free Press.

Roger WF (1950) A comparative study of the Wakefield prison population in 1948. I. *British journal of delinquency*, 1: 15–28.

Ross HE, Glaser FB, Germanson T (1988) The prevalence of psychiatric disorders in patients with alcohol and other drug problems. *Archives of general psychiatry*, 45: 1023.

Rounsaville BJ et al. (1991) Psychiatric diagnoses of treatment-seeking cocaine abusers. *Archives of general psychiatry*, 48: 43.

Runeson B, Beskow J (1991) Borderline personality disorder in young Swedish suicides. *Journal of nervous and mental disease*, 179:153.

Rutter M (1987) Temperament, personality and personality disorder. *British journal of psychiatry*, 150: 443–458.

Schneider K (1923) *Die Psychopathischen Personlichkeiten*. [Psychopathic personalities.] Berlin, Springer.

Schroeder ML, Livesley WJ (1991) An evaluation of DSM-III-R personality disorders. *Acta psychiatrica Scandinavica*, 84: 512–519.

Seivewright H et al. (1991) A three-year follow-up of psychiatric morbidity in urban and rural primary care. *Psychological medicine*, 21: 495–503.

Sethi BB et al. (1972) A psychiatric survey of 500 rural families. *Indian journal of psychiatry*, 14: 183–196.

Shea MT et al. (1990) Personality disorders and treatment outcome in the NIMH Treatment of Depression Collaborative Research Program. *American journal of psychiatry*, 147: 711–717.

Shepherd M et al. (1966) *Psychiatric illness in general practice*. Oxford, Oxford University Press.

Shepherd M, Sartorius N (1974) Personality disorder and the International Classification of Diseases. *Psychological medicine*, 4: 141–146.

Simonsen E, Mellergard M (1988) Trends in the use of the borderline diagnosis in Denmark from 1975 to 1985. *Journal of personality disorders*, 2: 102–108.

Sjobring H (1973) Personality structure and development: a model and its applications. *Acta psychiatrica Scandinavica*, Suppl. 244.

Skodol AE et al. (1988) Validating structured DSM-III-R personality disorder assessments with longitudinal data. *American journal of psychiatry*, 145: 1297–1299.

Smith GR et al. (1991) Antisocial personality disorder in primary care patients with somatization disorder. *Comprehensive psychiatry*, 32: 367–372.

Spitzer RL et al. (1991) Results of a survey of forensic psychiatrists on the validity of the sadistic personality disorder diagnosis. *American journal of psychiatry*, 148: 875–879.

Spitzer RL, Williams JBW (1987) *Structured Clinical Interview for DSM-III-R Personality Disorders (SCID-II)*. New York, New York State Psychiatric Institute, Biometric Research Department.

Stone MH, Stone DK, Hurst SW (1987) Natural history of borderline patients treated by intensive hospitalization. *Psychiatric clinics of North America*, 10: 185–206.

Stromgren E (1950) Statistical and genetic population studies within psychiatry: methods and principal results. In: *Congrès International de Psychiatrie, Paris VI, Psychiatrie Sociale.* [International Congress of Psychiatry, University of Paris VI, Social Psychiatry.] Paris, Hermann.

Swartz M et al. (1990) Estimating the prevalence of borderline personality disorder in the community. *Journal of personality disorders*, 4: 257–272.

Tarnopolsky A, Berelowitz M (1987) Borderline personality: a review of recent research. *British journal of psychiatry*, 151: 724–734.

Torgersen S (1985) Relationship of schizotypal personality disorder to schizophrenia. *Schizophrenia bulletin*, 11: 554–564.

Torgersen J (1989) Localizing DSM-III personality disorders in a three-dimensional space. *Journal of personality disorders*, 3: 274–281.

Turner SM et al. (1991) Social phobia: axis I and II correlates. *Journal of abnormal psychology*, 100: 102–106.

Tyrer P (1987a) Problems in the classification of personality disorder. *Psychological medicine*, 17: 15–20.

Tyrer P (1987b) Measurement of abnormal personality: a review. *Journal of the Royal Society of Medicine*, 80: 637–639.

Tyrer P (1990) Diagnosing personality disorders. *Current opinion in psychiatry*, 3: 182–187.

Tyrer P, Casey P, Ferguson B (1991) Personality disorder in perspective. *British journal of psychiatry*, 159: 463–471.

Tyrer P, Casey P, Gall J (1983) Relationship between neurosis and personality disorder. *British journal of psychiatry*, 142: 404–408.

Tyrer P et al. (1979) Reliability of a schedule for rating personality disorders. *British journal of psychiatry*, 135: 168–174.

Weissman MM (1993) The epidemiology of personality disorders: a 1990 update. *Journal of personality disorders*, 7: 44–62.

Weissman MM, Myers JK (1980) Psychiatric disorders in a US community. *Acta psychiatrica Scandinavica*, 62: 99–111.

Wells EJ et al. (1989) Christchurch psychiatric epidemiology study, Part I: Methodology and lifetime prevalence for specific psychiatric disorders. *Australian and New Zealand journal of psychiatry*, 23: 315–326.

WHO (1972) *The Seventh Seminar on Standardization of Psychiatric Diagnosis, Classification and Statistics of Personality Disorders and Drug Dependence, Tokyo, 8–14 December 1971.* (Unpublished document MNH/72.2; available on request from the Division of Mental Health, World Health Organization, 1211 Geneva 27, Switzerland.)

WHO (1977) *Manual of the International Statistical Classification of Diseases, Injuries, and Causes of Death, ninth revision.* Geneva, World Health Organization.

WHO (1992a) *The ICD-10 Classification of Mental and Behavioural Disorders. Clinical descriptions and diagnostic guidelines.* Geneva, World Health Organization (reprinted, 1993).

WHO (1992b) *The International Statistical Classification of Diseases and Related Health Problems, tenth revision. Volume 1: tabular list.* Geneva, World Health Organization.

WHO (1993) *The ICD-10 Classification of Mental and Behavioural Disorders. Diagnostic criteria for research.* Geneva, World Health Organization.

WHO (in press) *Lexicon of psychiatric and mental health terms*, 2nd ed. Geneva, World Health Organization.

Widiger TA (1987) *Personality Interview Questions II (PIQ-II).* Lexington, KY, University of Kentucky.

Widiger TA et al. (1986) Diagnostic criteria for the borderline and schizotypal personality disorders. *Journal of abnormal psychology*, 95: 43–51.

Widiger TA et al. (1987) A multidimensional scaling of the DSM-III personality disorders. *Acta psychiatrica Scandinavica*, 44: 557–563.

Widiger TA et al. (1988) DSM-III-R personality disorders: an overview. *American journal of psychiatry*, 145: 786–795.

Widiger TA et al. (1991) Toward an empirical classification for the DSM-IV. *Journal of abnormal psychology*, 100: 280–288.

Widiger TA, Frances A (1985a) Axis II personality disorders: diagnostic and treatment issues. *Hospital and community psychiatry*, 36: 619–627.

Widiger TA, Frances A (1985b) The DSM-III personality disorders: perspectives from psychology. *Archives of general psychiatry*, 42: 615–627.

Widiger TA, Rogers JH (1989) Prevalence and comorbidity of personality disorders. *Psychiatric annals*, 19: 132–136.

Widiger TA, Weissman MM (1991) Epidemiology of borderline personality disorder. *Hospital and community psychiatry*, 42: 1015–1021.

Zanarini MC (1983) *Diagnostic Interview for Personality Disorders (DIPD)*. Belmont, MA, McLean Hospital, Psychosocial Research Program.

Zanarini MC et al. (1987) The diagnostic interview for personality disorders: interrater and test-retest reliability. *Comprehensive psychiatry*, 28: 467–480.

Zimmerman M, Coryell WH (1990) Diagnosing personality disorders in the community. *Archives of general psychiatry*, 47: 527–531.

Zimmerman M et al. (1988) Diagnosing personality disorder in depressed patients. A comparison of patient and informant interviews. *Archives of general psychiatry*, 45: 733–737.

The ICD-10 Classification of Mental and Behavioural Disorders: clinical descriptions and diagnostic guidelines

F60–F62 Specific personality disorders, mixed and other personality disorders, and enduring personality changes

These types of condition comprise deeply ingrained and enduring behaviour patterns, manifesting themselves as inflexible responses to a broad range of personal and social situations. They represent either extreme or significant deviations from the way the average individual in a given culture perceives, thinks, feels, and particularly relates to others. Such behaviour patterns tend to be stable and to encompass multiple domains of behaviour and psychological functioning. They are frequently, but not always, associated with various degrees of subjective distress and problems in social functioning and performance.

Personality disorders differ from personality change in their timing and the mode of their emergence: they are developmental conditions, which appear in childhood or adolescence and continue into adulthood. They are not secondary to another mental disorder or brain disease, although they may precede and coexist with other disorders. In contrast, personality change is acquired, usually during adult life, following severe or prolonged stress, extreme environmental deprivation, serious psychiatric disorder, or brain disease or injury (personality change associated with the latter is classified under F07.–).

Each of the conditions in this group can be classified according to its predominant behavioural manifestations. However, classification in this area is currently limited to the description of a series of types and subtypes, which are not mutually exclusive and which overlap in some of their characteristics.

Personality disorders are therefore subdivided according to clusters of traits that correspond to the most frequent or conspicuous behavioural manifestations. The subtypes so described are recognized widely as major forms of personality deviation. In making a diagnosis of personality disorder, the clinician should consider all aspects of personal functioning, although the diagnostic formulation, to be simple and efficient, will refer to only those dimensions or traits for which the suggested thresholds for severity are reached.

The assessment should be based on as many sources of information as possible. Although it is sometimes possible to evaluate a personality condition in a single interview with the patient, it is often necessary to have more than one interview and to collect history data from informants.

Cyclothymia and schizotypal disorders were formerly classified with the personality disorders but are now listed elsewhere (cyclothymia in F30–F39 and schizotypal disorder in F20–F29), since they seem to have many aspects in common with the other disorders in those blocks (e.g. phenomena, family history).

The subdivision of personality change is based on the cause or antecedent of such change, i.e. catastrophic experience, prolonged stress or strain, and psychiatric illness (excluding residual schizophrenia, which is classified under F20.5).

It is important to separate personality conditions from the disorders included in other categories of this book. If a personality condition precedes or follows a time-limited or chronic psychiatric disorder, both should be diagnosed. Use of the multiaxial format accompanying the core classification of mental disorders and psychosocial factors will facilitate the recording of such conditions and disorders.

Cultural or regional variations in the manifestations of personality conditions are important, but specific knowledge in this area is still scarce. Personality conditions that appear to be frequently recognized in a given part of the world but do not correspond to any one of the specified subtypes below may be classified as "other" personality conditions and identified through a five-character code provided in an adaptation of this classification for that particular country or region. Local variations in the manifestations of a personality disorder may also be reflected in the wording of the diagnostic guidelines set for such conditions.

F60 Specific personality disorders

A specific personality disorder is a severe disturbance in the characterological constitution and behavioural tendencies of the individual, usually involving several areas of the personality, and nearly always associated with considerable personal and social disruption. Personality disorder tends to appear in late childhood or adolescence and continues to be manifest into adulthood. It is therefore unlikely that the diagnosis of personality disorder will be appropriate before the age of 16 or 17 years. General diagnostic guidelines applying to all personality disorders are presented below; supplementary descriptions are provided with each of the subtypes.

Diagnostic guidelines
Conditions not directly attributable to gross brain damage or disease, or to another psychiatric disorder, meeting the following criteria:

(a) markedly dysharmonious attitudes and behaviour, involving usually several areas of functioning, e.g. affectivity, arousal, impulse control, ways of perceiving and thinking, and style of relating to others;

(b) the abnormal behaviour pattern is enduring, of long standing, and not limited to episodes of mental illness;

(c) the abnormal behaviour pattern is pervasive and clearly maladaptive to a broad range of personal and social situations;

(d) the above manifestations always appear during childhood or adolescence and continue into adulthood;

(e) the disorder leads to considerable personal distress but this may only become apparent late in its course;

(f) the disorder is usually, but not invariably, associated with significant problems in occupational and social performance.

For different cultures it may be necessary to develop specific sets of criteria with regard to social norms, rules and obligations. For diagnosing most of the subtypes listed below, clear evidence is usually required of the presence of *at least three* of the traits or behaviours given in the clinical description.

F60.0 Paranoid personality disorder

Personality disorder characterized by:

(a) excessive sensitiveness to setbacks and rebuffs;

(b) tendency to bear grudges persistently, i.e. refusal to forgive insults and injuries or slights;

(c) suspiciousness and a pervasive tendency to distort experience by misconstruing the neutral or friendly actions of others as hostile or contemptuous;

(d) a combative and tenacious sense of personal rights out of keeping with the actual situation;

(e) recurrent suspicions, without justification, regarding sexual fidelity of spouse or sexual partner;

(f) a tendency to experience excessive self-importance, manifest in a persistent self-referential attitude;

(g) preoccupation with unsubstantiated "conspiratorial" explanations of events both immediate to the patient and in the world at large.

Includes: expansive paranoid, fanatic, querulant and sensitive paranoid personality (disorder)

Excludes: delusional disorder (F22.–)
schizophrenia (F20.–)

F60.1 Schizoid personality disorder

Personality disorder meeting the following description:

(a) few, if any, activities provide pleasure;

(b) emotional coldness, detachment or flattened affectivity;

(c) limited capacity to express either warm, tender feelings or anger towards others;

(d) apparent indifference to either praise or criticism;

(e) little interest in having sexual experiences with another person (taking into account age);

(f) almost invariable preference for solitary activities;
(g) excessive preoccupation with fantasy and introspection;
(h) lack of close friends or confiding relationships (or having only one) and of desire for such relationships;
(i) marked insensitivity to prevailing social norms and conventions.

Excludes: Asperger's syndrome (F84.5)
   delusional disorder (F22.0)
   schizoid disorder of childhood (F84.5)
   schizophrenia (F20.–)
   schizotypal disorder (F21)

F60.2 Dissocial personality disorder

Personality disorder, usually coming to attention because of a gross disparity between behaviour and the prevailing social norms, and characterized by:

(a) callous unconcern for the feelings of others;
(b) gross and persistent attitude of irresponsibility and disregard for social norms, rules and obligations;
(c) incapacity to maintain enduring relationships, though having no difficulty in establishing them;
(d) very low tolerance to frustration and a low threshold for discharge of aggression, including violence;
(e) incapacity to experience guilt and to profit from experience, particularly punishment;
(f) marked proneness to blame others, or to offer plausible rationalizations, for the behaviour that has brought the patient into conflict with society.

There may also be persistent irritability as an associated feature. Conduct disorder during childhood and adolescence, though not invariably present, may further support the diagnosis.

Includes: amoral, antisocial, asocial, psychopathic, and sociopathic personality (disorder)

Excludes: conduct disorders (F91.–)
   emotionally unstable personality disorder (F60.3)

F60.3 Emotionally unstable personality disorder

A personality disorder in which there is a marked tendency to act impulsively without consideration of the consequences, together with affective instability. The ability to plan ahead may be minimal, and outbursts of intense anger may often lead to violence or "behavioural explosions"; these are easily precipitated when impulsive acts are criticized or thwarted by others. Two variants of this personality disorder are specified, and both share this general theme of impulsiveness and lack of self-control.

F60.30 Impulsive type

The predominant characteristics are emotional instability and lack of impulse control. Outbursts of violence or threatening behaviour are common, particularly in response to criticism by others.

Includes: explosive and aggressive personality (disorder)

Excludes: dissocial personality disorder (F60.2)

F60.31 Borderline type

Several of the characteristics of emotional instability are present; in addition, the patient's own self-image, aims, and internal preferences (including sexual) are often unclear or disturbed. There are usually chronic feelings of emptiness. A liability to become involved in intense and unstable relationships may cause repeated emotional crises and may be associated with excessive efforts to avoid abandonment and a series of suicidal threats or acts of self-harm (although these may occur without obvious precipitants).

Includes: borderline personality (disorder)

F60.4 Histrionic personality disorder

Personality disorder characterized by:

(a) self-dramatization, theatricality, exaggerated expression of emotions;
(b) suggestibility, easily influenced by others or by circumstances;
(c) shallow and labile affectivity;
(d) continually seeking for excitement and activities in which the patient is the centre of attention;
(e) inappropriate seductiveness in appearance or behaviour;
(f) over-concern with physical attractiveness.

Associated features may include egocentricity, self-indulgence, continuous longing for appreciation, feelings that are easily hurt, and persistent manipulative behaviour to achieve own needs.

Includes: hysterical and psychoinfantile personality (disorder)

F60.5 Anankastic personality disorder

Personality disorder characterized by:

(a) feelings of excessive doubt and caution;
(b) preoccupation with details, rules, lists, order, organization or schedule;
(c) perfectionism that interferes with task completion;
(d) excessive conscientiousness, scrupulousness, and undue preoccupation with productivity to the exclusion of pleasure and interpersonal relationships;
(e) excessive pedantry and adherence to social conventions;
(f) rigidity and stubbornness;

(g) unreasonable insistence by the patient that others submit to exactly his or her way of doing things, or unreasonable reluctance to allow others to do things;

(h) intrusion of insistent and unwelcome thoughts or impulses.

Includes: compulsive and obsessional personality (disorder)
obsessive–compulsive personality disorder

F60.6 Anxious [avoidant] personality disorder
Personality disorder characterized by:

(a) persistent and pervasive feelings of tension and apprehension;
(b) belief that one is socially inept, personally unappealing, or inferior to others;
(c) excessive preoccupation with being criticized or rejected in social situations;
(d) unwillingness to get involved with people unless certain of being liked;
(e) restrictions in lifestyle because of need to have physical security;
(f) avoidance of social or occupational activities that involve significant interpersonal contact because of fear of criticism, disapproval, or rejection.

Associated features may include hypersensitivity to rejection and criticism.

F60.7 Dependent personality disorder
Personality disorder characterized by:

(a) encouraging or allowing others to make most of one's important life decisions;
(b) subordination of one's own needs to those of others on whom one is dependent, and undue compliance with their wishes;
(c) unwillingness to make even reasonable demands on the people one depends on;
(d) feeling uncomfortable or helpless when alone, because of exaggerated fears of inability to care for oneself;
(e) preoccupation with fears of being abandoned by a person with whom one has a close relationship, and of being left to care for oneself;
(f) limited capacity to make everyday decisions without an excessive amount of advice and reassurance from others.

Associated features may include perceiving oneself as helpless, incompetent, and lacking stamina.

Includes: asthenic, inadequate, passive, and self-defeating personality (disorder)

F60.8 Other specific personality disorders
A personality disorder that fits none of the specific rubrics F60.0–F60.7.

Includes: eccentric, "haltlose" type, immature, narcissistic, passive–aggressive, and psychoneurotic personality (disorder)

F60.9 Personality disorder, unspecified

Includes: character neurosis NOS
pathological personality NOS

The ICD-10 Classification of Mental and Behavioural Disorders: diagnostic criteria for research

F60–F62 Specific personality disorders, mixed and other personality disorders, and enduring personality changes

F60 Specific personality disorders

G1. There is evidence that the individual's characteristic and enduring patterns of inner experience and behaviour as a whole deviate markedly from the culturally expected and accepted range (or "norm"). Such deviation must be manifest in more than one of the following areas:

(1) cognition (i.e. ways of perceiving and interpreting things, people, and events; forming attitudes and images of self and others);

(2) affectivity (range, intensity, and appropriateness of emotional arousal and response);

(3) control over impulses and gratification of needs;

(4) manner of relating to others and of handling interpersonal situations.

G2. The deviation must manifest itself pervasively as behaviour that is inflexible, maladaptive, or otherwise dysfunctional across a broad range of personal and social situations (i.e. not being limited to one specific "triggering" stimulus or situation).

G3. There is personal distress, or adverse impact on the social environment, or both, clearly attributable to the behaviour referred to in criterion G2.

G4. There must be evidence that the deviation is stable and of long duration, having its onset in late childhood or adolescence.

G5. The deviation cannot be explained as a manifestation or consequence of other adult mental disorders, although episodic or chronic conditions from sections F00–F59 or F70–F79 of this classification may coexist with, or be superimposed upon, the deviation.

G6. Organic brain disease, injury, or dysfunction must be excluded as the possible cause of the deviation. (If an organic causation is demonstrable, category F07–. should be used).

Comments. The assessment of criteria G1–G6 above should be based on as many sources of information as possible. Although it is sometimes possible to obtain sufficient evidence from a single interview with the individual, as a general rule it is recommended to have more than one interview with the person and to collect history data from informants or past records.

It is suggested that sub-criteria should be developed to define behaviour patterns specific to different cultural settings concerning social norms, rules, and obligations where needed (such as examples of irresponsibility and disregard of social norms in dissocial personality disorder).

The diagnosis of personality disorder for research purposes requires the identification of a subtype. (More than one subtype can be coded if there is compelling evidence that the subject meets multiple sets of criteria.)

F60.0 Paranoid personality disorder

A. The general criteria for personality disorder (F60) must be met.

B. At least four of the following must be present:

(1) excessive sensitivity to setbacks and rebuffs;
(2) tendency to bear grudges persistently, e.g. refusal to forgive insults, injuries, or slights;
(3) suspiciousness and a pervasive tendency to distort experience by misconstruing the neutral or friendly actions of others as hostile or contemptuous;
(4) a combative and tenacious sense of personal rights out of keeping with the actual situation;
(5) recurrent suspicions, without justification, regarding sexual fidelity of spouse or sexual partner;
(6) persistent self-referential attitude, associated particularly with excessive self-importance;
(7) preoccupation with unsubstantiated "conspiratorial" explanations of events either immediate to the patient or in the world at large.

F60.1 Schizoid personality disorder

A. The general criteria for personality disorder (F60) must be met.

B. At least four of the following must be present:

(1) few, if any, activities provide pleasure;
(2) display of emotional coldness, detachment, or flattened affectivity;
(3) limited capacity to express either warm, tender feelings or anger towards others;
(4) an appearance of indifference to either praise or criticism;

(5) little interest in having sexual experiences with another person (taking into account age);

(6) consistent choice of solitary activities;

(7) excessive preoccupation with fantasy and introspection;

(8) no desire for, or possession of, any close friends or confiding relationships (or only one);

(9) marked insensitivity to prevailing social norms and conventions; disregard for such norms and conventions is unintentional.

F60.2 Dissocial personality disorder

A. The general criteria for personality disorder (F60) must be met.

B. At least three of the following must be present:

(1) callous unconcern for the feelings of others;

(2) gross and persistent attitude of irresponsibility and disregard for social norms, rules, and obligations;

(3) incapacity to maintain enduring relationships, though with no difficulty in establishing them;

(4) very low tolerance to frustration and a low threshold for discharge of aggression, including violence;

(5) incapacity to experience guilt, or to profit from adverse experience, particularly punishment;

(6) marked proneness to blame others, or to offer plausible rationalizations for the behaviour that has brought the individual into conflict with society.

Comments. Persistent irritability and the presence of conduct disorder during childhood and adolescence complete the clinical picture but are not required for the diagnosis.

It is suggested that sub-criteria should be developed to define behaviour patterns specific to different cultural settings concerning social norms, rules, and obligations where needed (such as examples of irresponsibility and disregard of social norms).

F60.3 Emotionally unstable personality disorder

F60.30 Impulsive type

A. The general criteria for personality disorder (F60) must be met.

B. At least three of the following must be present, one of which must be (2):

(1) marked tendency to act unexpectedly and without consideration of the consequences;

(2) marked tendency to quarrelsome behaviour and to conflicts with others, especially when impulsive acts are thwarted or criticized;

(3) liability to outbursts of anger or violence, with inability to control the resulting behavioural explosions;

(4) difficulty in maintaining any course of action that offers no immediate reward;

(5) unstable and capricious mood.

F60.31 Borderline type

A. The general criteria for personality disorder (F60) must be met.

B. At least three of the symptoms mentioned in criterion B for F60.30 must be present, with at least two of the following in addition:

(1) disturbances in and uncertainty about self-image, aims, and internal preferences (including sexual);

(2) liability to become involved in intense and unstable relationships, often leading to emotional crises;

(3) excessive efforts to avoid abandonment;

(4) recurrent threats or acts of self-harm;

(5) chronic feelings of emptiness.

F60.4 Histrionic personality disorder

A. The general criteria for personality disorder (F60) must be met.

B. At least four of the following must be present:

(1) self-dramatization, theatricality, or exaggerated expression of emotions;

(2) suggestibility (the individual is easily influenced by others or by circumstances);

(3) shallow and labile affectivity;

(4) continual seeking for excitement and activities in which the individual is the centre of attention;

(5) inappropriate seductiveness in appearance or behaviour;

(6) over-concern with physical attractiveness.

Comments. Egocentricity, self-indulgence, continuous longing for appreciation, lack of consideration for others, feelings that are easily hurt, and persistent manipulative behaviour complete the clinical picture, but are not required for the diagnosis.

F60.5 Anankastic personality disorder

Note: This disorder is often referred to as obsessive–compulsive personality disorder.

A. The general criteria for personality disorder (F60) must be met.

B. At least four of the following must be present:

(1) feelings of excessive doubt and caution;

(2) preoccupation with details, rules, lists, order, organization, or schedule;

(3) perfectionism that interferes with task completion;

(4) excessive conscientiousness and scrupulousness;

(5) undue preoccupation with productivity to the exclusion of pleasure and interpersonal relationships;

(6) excessive pedantry and adherence to social conventions;

(7) rigidity and stubbornness;

(8) unreasonable insistence by the individual that others submit to exactly his or her way of doing things, or unreasonable reluctance to allow others to do things.

F60.6 Anxious [avoidant] personality disorder

A. The general criteria for personality disorder (F60) must be met.

B. At least four of the following must be present:

(1) persistent and pervasive feelings of tension and apprehension;

(2) belief that one is socially inept, personally unappealing, or inferior to others;

(3) excessive preoccupation with being criticized or rejected in social situations;

(4) unwillingness to become involved with people unless certain of being liked;

(5) restrictions in lifestyle because of need for physical security;

(6) avoidance of social or occupational activities that involve significant interpersonal contact, because of fear of criticism, disapproval or rejection.

F60.7 Dependent personality disorder

A. The general criteria for personality disorder (F60) must be met.

B. At least four of the following must be present:

(1) encouraging or allowing others to make most of one's important life decisions;

(2) subordination of one's own needs to those of others on whom one is dependent, and undue compliance with their wishes;

(3) unwillingness to make even reasonable demands on the people one depends on;

(4) feeling uncomfortable or helpless when alone, because of exaggerated fears of inability to care for oneself;

(5) preoccupation with fears of being left to care for oneself;

(6) limited capacity to make everyday decisions without an excessive amount of advice and reassurance from others.

F60.8 Other specific personality disorders

If none of the preceding rubrics is fitting, but a condition meeting the general criteria for personality disorder listed under F60 is nevertheless present, this code should be used. An extra character may be added for identifying specific personality disorders not currently in ICD-10. In using code F60.8, it is recommended always to record a vignette description of the specific disorder.

F60.9 Personality disorder, unspecified